OAuth 2.0 Identity and Access Management Patterns

A practical hands-on guide to implementing secure API
authorization flow scenarios with OAuth 2.0

Martin Spasovski

BIRMINGHAM - MUMBAI

OAuth 2.0 Identity and Access Management Patterns

First published: November 2013

Production Reference: 1181113

Published by Packt Publishing Ltd.
Livery Place
35 Livery Street
Birmingham B3 2PB, UK..

ISBN 978-1-78328-559-4

www.packtpub.com

Cover Image by Abhishek Pandey (abhishek.pandey1210@gmail.com)

Credits

Author
Martin Spasovski

Reviewers
Charles Bihis
Max Countryman

Acquisition Editor
Vinay Argekar

Commissioning Editor
Mohammed Fahad

Technical Editors
Rosmy George
Arwa Manasawala

Project Coordinator
Amigya Khurana
Akash Poojary

Proofreader
Lawrence A. Herman

Indexer
Mehreen Deshmukh

Graphics
Yuvraj Mannari
Abhinash Sahu

Production Coordinator
Melwyn D'sa

Cover Work
Melwyn D'sa

About the Author

Martin Spasovski is a software development professional involved in developing JVM-based enterprise solutions. He has been working with various back-end technologies and architectures, and with various front-end technologies (from RCP to modern JavaScript web applications), and knows how to integrate both sides well. He mostly likes to work in the domain of data processing, software optimization, and providing custom solutions.

He is a vocal open source and open standards supporter, and a member of the local Java User Group named JUGMK, and likes to research on emerging technologies and give internal presentations at Seavus, the company that he works for.

He can be found at `http://thisismartin.com`, where his blog, contact info, and links to public project repositories can be found.

I'd like to thank the team at Packt Publishing for giving me the opportunity to write this book and for their guidance. I'd also like to thank my close ones (Biljana, Stefan, and my parents) for the support given and enthusiasm shared.

About the Reviewers

Charles Bihis is a technologist and entrepreneur. He earned his degree in computer science from The University of British Columbia, where he specialized in software engineering. He is known for his open source contributions as well as his work in the identity space. His areas of interest include algorithms and data structures, graph theory, and distributed systems. He is currently working as a Computer Scientist at Adobe Systems where he focuses on solving the latest problems in the identity and security space. You can reach him through his website at www.whoischarles.com.

Max Countryman is a polyglot, full-stack programmer with extensive experience in building highly-available web server applications. He is an active member of the Python and Clojure communities and spends his free time working on open source projects.

www.PacktPub.com

Support files, eBooks, discount offers and more

You might want to visit www.PacktPub.com for support files and downloads related to your book.

Did you know that Packt offers eBook versions of every book published, with PDF and ePub files available? You can upgrade to the eBook version at www.PacktPub.com and as a print book customer, you are entitled to a discount on the eBook copy. Get in touch with us at service@packtpub.com for more details.

At www.PacktPub.com, you can also read a collection of free technical articles, sign up for a range of free newsletters and receive exclusive discounts and offers on Packt books and eBooks.

http://PacktLib.PacktPub.com

Do you need instant solutions to your IT questions? PacktLib is Packt's online digital book library. Here, you can access, read and search across Packt's entire library of books.

Why Subscribe?

- Fully searchable across every book published by Packt
- Copy and paste, print and bookmark content
- On demand and accessible via web browser

Free Access for Packt account holders

If you have an account with Packt at www.PacktPub.com, you can use this to access PacktLib today and view nine entirely free books. Simply use your login credentials for immediate access.

Table of Contents

Preface

OAuth 2.0 has become the most widely used authorization framework. From securing service APIs to providing an easy to use sign-in mechanism, it provides a protection layer for the assets of the users so that various third party applications cannot have direct access to them. From service providers such as Amazon and social media platforms such as Facebook and Twitter to various internal enterprise solutions, OAuth 2.0 is often the authorization standard of choice.

OAuth 2.0 Identity and Access Management Patterns is a practical and informative book that will help you learn what OAuth 2.0 is, how to handle and implement various authorization flows for the chosen type of application, which security precautions to take into consideration, and so on.

You will explore each type of application such as web, client side, desktop, and so called trusted applications, and will see how to implement various authorization grant flows for each type of application. You will explore practical code examples that are executable as standalone applications running on top of Spring MVC. You will learn about the security features that are part of OAuth 2.0, what information that is transmitted during the execution of a flow is to be protected, and which precautions can be made. You will also learn how to use SAML 2.0 assertions in order to provide additional security. In the end, you will also learn which tools and libraries are there for the popular programming languages that provide support for integration with OAuth 2.0.

What this book covers

Chapter 1, Need for OAuth 2.0, introduces OAuth 2.0, what purpose it has, why was it created, and what the benefits of its use are.

Chapter 2, Terms You Need to Know, explains key terminology used and defined in the OAuth 2.0 specification.

Chapter 3, First Step for Your Application, covers client registration, a mandatory step that has to be done when developing an OAuth client application.

Chapter 4, OAuth for Web Server Applications, explains what web server applications are and how OAuth 2.0 is used in them by applying the authorization code grant. The grant is covered in detail and a practical code example of a client application is made.

Chapter 5, OAuth for Client-side Applications, explains what client-side applications are and how OAuth 2.0 is used in them by applying the implicit grant. The grant is covered in detail and a practical code example of a client application is made.

Chapter 6, OAuth for Mobile Applications, explains how OAuth 2.0 is used in mobile applications, which OAuth grants can be used and in which way, and gives out instructions for Android and iOS.

Chapter 7, OAuth for Trusted Applications, explains what trusted applications are and covers the Resource Owner Password Credentials grant and the client credentials grant in detail. Additionally, it explains how to perform authorization requests for these grants together with practical code examples.

Chapter 8, Security Considerations, explains what data is to be protected during an execution of a grant flow, what features OAuth 2.0 contains regarding information security, and which precautions should be taken into consideration.

Chapter 9, Additional Security with SAML, explains how to use SAML 2.0 assertions as a means of providing additional security when doing client authentication or when requesting an access token with OAuth 2.0.

Chapter 10, Common Tools and Libraries, covers the tools and libraries available for application developers.

Appendix, OAuth 2.0 Resources, provides resources useful for those interested in further expanding their knowledge in OAuth 2.0 or getting involved in future specification development.

What you need for this book

The latest Java JDK 7 and Apache Maven 3.0 or above are required for executing the code examples. The latest Java JDK 6 will execute the examples just fine, but an update to the newest one is recommended because updates for this version are no longer provided. Another important thing to mention is that, when installing the JDK, the Java browser plugin is not required and doesn't have to be installed. Additionally, a source code editor (for example, Notepad++, Geany, jEdit, or any other) for editing and browsing the examples is needed.

Who this book is for

This book is for software application developers, software architects, and enthusiasts in the OAuth 2.0 framework. It is for those that want to understand the inner workings of OAuth 2.0 and/or need to implement an authorization flow for an application. Additionally, it is for those that want to know how to make OAuth 2.0 client applications more secure.

Conventions

In this book, you will find a number of styles of text that distinguish between different kinds of information. Here are some examples of these styles, and an explanation of their meaning.

Code words in text, database table names, folder names, filenames, file extensions, path names, dummy URLs, user input, and Twitter handles are shown as follows: "Some may return a `userId` parameter, representing some internal identifier for the user that has authorized the request."

A block of code is set as follows:

```
{
    "access_token":"exampleAccessTokenValue",
    "expires_in":3600,
    "scope":"exampleScopeValue",
    "state":"exampleStateValue",
    "refresh_token":"exampleRefreshTokenValue"
}
```

New terms and **important words** are shown in bold. Words that you see on the screen, in menus or dialog boxes for example, appear in the text like this: "What we see in the previous screenshot are the client ID and client secret, named as **App ID** and **App Secret**."

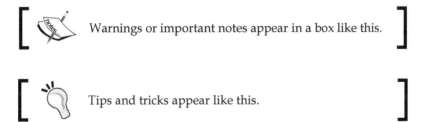

Warnings or important notes appear in a box like this.

Tips and tricks appear like this.

Reader feedback

Feedback from our readers is always welcome. Let us know what you think about this book—what you liked or may have disliked. Reader feedback is important for us to develop titles that you really get the most out of.

To send us general feedback, simply send an e-mail to feedback@packtpub.com, and mention the book title via the subject of your message.

If there is a topic that you have expertise in and you are interested in either writing or contributing to a book, see our author guide on www.packtpub.com/authors.

Customer support

Now that you are the proud owner of a Packt book, we have a number of things to help you to get the most from your purchase.

Downloading the example code

You can download the example code files for all Packt books you have purchased from your account at http://www.packtpub.com. If you purchased this book elsewhere, you can visit http://www.packtpub.com/support and register to have the files e-mailed directly to you.

Errata

Although we have taken every care to ensure the accuracy of our content, mistakes do happen. If you find a mistake in one of our books—maybe a mistake in the text or the code—we would be grateful if you would report this to us. By doing so, you can save other readers from frustration and help us improve subsequent versions of this book. If you find any errata, please report them by visiting http://www.packtpub.com/submit-errata, selecting your book, clicking on the **errata submission form** link, and entering the details of your errata. Once your errata are verified, your submission will be accepted and the errata will be uploaded on our website, or added to any list of existing errata, under the Errata section of that title. Any existing errata can be viewed by selecting your title from http://www.packtpub.com/support.

Piracy

Piracy of copyright material on the Internet is an ongoing problem across all media. At Packt, we take the protection of our copyright and licenses very seriously. If you come across any illegal copies of our works, in any form, on the Internet, please provide us with the location address or website name immediately so that we can pursue a remedy.

Please contact us at `copyright@packtpub.com` with a link to the suspected pirated material.

We appreciate your help in protecting our authors, and our ability to bring you valuable content.

Questions

You can contact us at `questions@packtpub.com` if you are having a problem with any aspect of the book, and we will do our best to address it.

1
Need for OAuth 2.0

OAuth 2.0 can be perceived as a protective layer for a given service, so that the client applications that are built for the service can have a standardized method of requesting the protected resources that belong to a user who uses the system, or resources that belong to the service in general. These resources may vary from various data that the user has stored, to various **application programming interface (API)** methods for system maintenance and more. The client applications, in order to obtain these protected resources, make HTTP requests to the predefined service endpoints and supply an access token— a token that says which user has approved the client application to access its data. OAuth 2.0 is a protocol that has found its place as an authorization framework in various services that are provided to clients, most commonly securing RESTful APIs and web-based applications. Additionally, when businesses want to communicate to other businesses purely by exchanging resources via services in a B2B manner, OAuth 2.0 can be used.

The OAuth 2.0 specification is fully named "The OAuth 2.0 Authorization Framework". It outlines the OAuth 2.0 protocol and leaves some points to be flexible and implemented in various ways; that's why it is important not to confuse it with a framework as in a technology stack; the term framework here means that the protocol can be implemented in various ways.

There are more cases, but what is evident is that OAuth 2.0 is able to handle the authorization layer in systems, providing access to protected resources in various scenarios, environments, and devices. Additionally, when it provides access, it does that on behalf of someone (most commonly the resource owner)—who is identified by the access token. But more details later.

More and more enterprises started using OAuth 1.0 and migrated to OAuth 2.0, from payment services such as PayPal and service providers such as Amazon to social media platforms, such as Facebook and Twitter, and various internal enterprise solutions. It's used in various scenarios, from securing service APIs to providing an easy-to-use sign-in mechanism and more. What we can notice is that OAuth 2.0 is found in enterprises in two ways: they use it and/or they support it. When enterprises consume protected resources from other service providers that are secured with OAuth 2.0, we say they use it (they may do the same internally between their own systems). Additionally, when enterprises secure their own services with OAuth 2.0 or provide OAuth-based solutions so that other enterprises can secure their services, we say they support it.

Why OAuth 2.0?

As the usage increased, developers ran into some common problems during the implementation phase, for both service providers and client applications. In OAuth 1.0, the use of cryptographic functions are a part of the protocol, which adds to the difficulty of the developers implementing it. Later on a security flaw was discovered, which had to be resolved, and resulted in a revised specification named OAuth 1.0a. Previous specifications also had a bad design decision. The use of **Secure Sockets Layer (SSL)** in order to secure data transfer between the parties that are part of the authorization flow was not mandatory, which meant sensitive information could be exposed.

Additionally, there were use cases that were not defined and could have been like the various authorization flows that are part of OAuth 2.0. It was evident that improvements could be made to the original OAuth 1.0 specification.

Development took off to define a new revised specification, versioned 2.0, authored by a bigger team and based on their experience in OAuth 1.0 implementations and deployments, on comments from the wider community, and on the additional OAuth 1.0 based specifications that were created meanwhile (and had the common goal of adding additional capabilities that were needed but not available in OAuth 1.0).

This resulted in the OAuth 2.0 authorization framework, delivering key improvements especially by simplifying and defining more clearly the way client developers should implement authorization against providers, in order to access protected resources.

OAuth 2.0 is not backwards compatible with 1.0, as they don't share a lot of similarities in implementation details, and they differ in the structure of exchanged information.

Therefore, developers that have worked with OAuth 1.0 should not make assumptions about OAuth 2.0 without getting familiar with it in the first place. Implementations for both 1.0 and 2.0 can co-exist for a given provider if it is chosen to support both, due to legacy clients, for example.

Support from service providers is leaning towards OAuth 2.0. A rough estimate of the percentage between providers that support OAuth 2.0 compared to OAuth 1.0 shows that at least 60 percent are in favor of OAuth 2.0. Some exclusively support OAuth 2.0 (a notable example of this is Facebook with its Graph API), some support OAuth 2.0 and announced deprecation of OAuth 1.0 (for example, Google), and some service providers support both versions.

Benefits of OAuth 2.0

To have a glimpse into the benefits, without going technical (which is the point in the next chapters), several scenarios follow.

API security

Imagine an enterprise providing an API for some customers (be it RESTful, SOAP-based, and so on). In order to make it secure and to have regulated access to it, one way is to use the so called basic authentication, where the username and password are sent using Base64 encoding—but not encoded or hashed—and **SSL** is used to secure the data transfer. The drawback here is that, in this type of authentication, the user, alongside his username, enters and sends his password over the wire as well.

What can be improved? In order to secure the API with OAuth 2.0, every time a request is made to the API, instead of username and password, an access token is sent. This token is obtained by the client application before making the requests, and represents the user on whose behalf the client application is using the API.

Related scenario—a client application, which is using the API, starts misbehaving and uses it improperly. All that has to be done is to revoke the access token, making all future requests invalid (if they are made with the same token).

Another important thing to note is that the access token can be set on how much access to have, which is called scope. So a client application may not have full API access when using access tokens. In contrast, if the client application was using username and password instead of access tokens, and these credentials were stolen, the whole API could be misused until the hijacked account is blocked.

Internal enterprise applications

Next, imagine a company utilizing a set of enterprise applications that are used internally. Company employees have to enter username and password manually in every separate application. This poses a security risk in several areas; there are several databases storing passwords, passwords are more often sent over, and so on.

With OAuth 2.0 what can be done is to have one application where the user logs in with his username and password (the OAuth 2.0 based service provider), and in all the other applications he is simply redirected to the provider where he logged in and confirms that he wants to be authorized. This way, instead of storing passwords these applications are storing the tokens for the users. The benefit is that when a password is stolen, the user has to reset his password, compared to when a token is stolen and it is revoked (invalidated).

Another related scenario is security in **BYOD (bring your own device)** companies. If a user brings his smartphone and uses an internal company application on it, and this smartphone gets stolen or compromised, the password of the user won't be exposed and only the tokens that were in use will have to be invalidated. The user can get a new device, and when he authorizes it he will get a new token.

Service integration and authorization delegation

Imagine that a user has an account on a photo sharing service, and also on a print ordering service.

If these two services have OAuth 2.0 integration between them, the user can authorize the printing service to access resources from the photo sharing service on his behalf. For example, the user would log in to the photo sharing service, then would log in to the printing service and request the integration, after which the user is redirected back to the photo sharing service, where he approves the authorization request.

From this point on, the printing service has an access token on behalf of this user, and can be aware which photos the user has uploaded. And the user can access the photos on the printing service without re-uploading them again there, but retrieved via the photo sharing service.

The best part of it is that the user hasn't given the username and password combination to the printing service, but instead the printing service has received an access token when it was authorized by the user.

This shows one of the key strengths of using OAuth 2.0 — authorization delegation. With OAuth 2.0 you can give access to your data/resources on some service to another one, and easily revoke this access when you change your mind. This applies everywhere, from internal enterprise applications to various services such as social media applications.

Federated identity

Another key strength of OAuth 2.0 is federated identity.

With federated identity, a person's digital identity and details (such as e-mail, name and surname, and gender) can be linked between several distinct services.

The previous two examples show this, but let's see another example; users can log in to one OAuth 2.0 provider (for example, Facebook or LinkedIn) and then log into other web services via this provider, without entering new username and password. For example, a user wants to leave a comment on some blog post and needs to be identified in order for the comment to be accepted.

This case is also known as using OAuth 2.0 for authentication. The client application (for example, the blogging platform) is requesting only the user's information after it got authorized and nothing more.

Easier service monitoring

Last but not least, enterprises can track and monitor more easily which access token is making which request; based on this they can make calculations and gain better insight about which services are used more often by its clients, and make optimizations.

Summary

In this chapter, we have learned what OAuth 2.0 is, what purpose it has, why it was created, and what the benefits of using it are.

In the next chapter, we will define and explain all key terms that are part of the OAuth 2.0 protocol.

2
Terms You Need To Know

In this chapter, we will define and explain all key terms, which will help us go through OAuth better. This chapter is important go to through before proceeding to later chapters.

Here, first we will learn which roles are defined in OAuth 2.0 and what is their purpose. After that are tokens, which types there are, and what they do. We'll also learn everything about the ones who are making the requests to the protected resources, the clients, and at the end of this chapter we'll learn about endpoints and access scope.

Roles

Let's take a look at the following sentence: OAuth 2.0 provides authorization so that a client (for example, a mobile photo viewer application) can make authorized requests to protected resources on a service (for example, user's photographs on an online storage service) on behalf of the resource owner (for example, the user who uploaded the photos). We'll keep this in mind as an example while learning which roles there are in this chapter.

Resource owner

A resource owner is an entity who is capable of granting access to a protected resource. When this entity is a person the term **end user** or **user** can be used as well.

Authorization server

In order for a client to access protected resources, this must first be authorized by the resource owner.

This is what the authorization server does—it asks the user (resource owner) for confirmation that the client should be authorized to have access. For every successful authorization request, the server issues the client a so called 'access token.' It is a token that the client uses to specify for which user it is making the requests. Additionally, the issued token is specific to the authorized client application, so it can be said that the access token represents the relation between the authorization server, the client application, and the resource owner. Moreover, some other parameters are sent along with the access token, and we will check them out later in this chapter.

Resource server

A resource server is the one who serves the protected resources, which are to be accessed by making authorized requests from a client application.

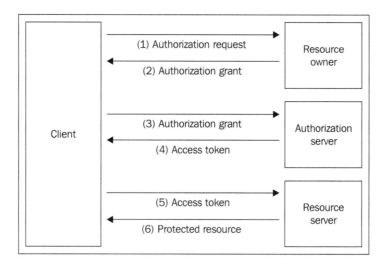

How the authorization and resource servers communicate is outside the scope of the OAuth 2.0 specification and therefore there are different implementations in the real world. They can be on separate servers, they can be on the same server, one authorization server can be used for several resource servers, and so on.

Client

A client is an application that makes requests to protected resources on the resource server, on behalf of the resource owner (the user).

A **client application** can be a web application, desktop application, mobile application, and so on. The OAuth 2.0 specification does not impose limitations regarding the environment on which the client application should run.

 From OAuth 2.0 's point of view it's important to associate the term client with the client application, and the term user with the resource owner, and not to mix them (here they are not interchangeable).

Authorization flow

Next we'll cover an abstract example of the authorization flow and describe in brief the actual ones that are defined in OAuth 2.0.

Abstract example

Now that we know the roles, we can recall the previous diagram, which shows an abstract example of the way a client gets authorized, gets the token, and makes requests to the protected resources on behalf of the user.

The first and the second step specify the interaction between the client and the resource owner:

- The client makes a request to the owner for authorization to his protected resources
- The owner approves the request (access granted) and the client receives an **Authorization grant** — credentialed data containing information about the owner's authorization

Generally the client does not ask the owner directly, and this is done with the assistance of the authorization server.

The third and the fourth step specifies the interaction between the client and the authorization server:

- The client supplies the authorization grant he got previously to the authorization server, so that he'll get an access token in response

- The authorization server checks the authorization grant and if it is valid the authorization server gives the client an access token

It is worth mentioning that the client also has to successfully authenticate with the server. So, in order to get an access token, the server not only checks the validity of the authorization grant but he first identifies who the client is.

This process of getting an authorization grant is discussed in detail later in this book. In this chapter we will just have a brief look at the four 'grant types' defined in the OAuth 2.0 specification — grant flow scenarios that cover various scenarios for desktop clients, web clients, mobile clients, and so on.

The last two steps, five and six, specify the interaction between the client and the resource server:

- The client makes a request specifying which protected resource he wants to access, and supplies the access token in order to pass security authentication

- The server checks if the access token is valid and fulfills the request if it is

OAuth 2.0 grant flows

One of the major improvements in OAuth 2.0 compared to OAuth 1.0 is the definition of various grant flows. Each flow has its use case and is recommended in some type of scenario, so let's go through a brief overview of them:

- **Authorization code grant flow**: This is used for web server applications in general and it's the most frequently used grant

- **Implicit grant flow**: This is used for client applications that are not capable of keeping the credentials secure and it is frequently used for applications that need read-only access to some data

- **Resource owner password credentials grant flow**: This is the only grant flow where the actual username and password from the resource owner (the user) are sent in exchange for an access token and it is frequently used in scenarios where an already existing solution is migrating over to OAuth 2.0

- **Client credentials grant flow**: This is used for client applications that want to request access to some service provider on behalf of themselves and not on behalf of some end user, and it is useful when in need to access some service APIs that are 'userless' (for example, for maintenance, statistics, and so on)

Tokens

There are two types of tokens in OAuth 2.0, the access token and the refresh token. The access token is the one that is used by the client application when making the requests to protected resources, and the refresh token is the one that is used to renew the access token when it is expired.

Access token

The first thing a client must do in order to access protected resources is to obtain an access token. Or in other words, a client application first has to be authorized by the user.

When the user authorizes an application, in the end the authorization server gives the client an access token. This token is associated with the user and is used as authorization credentials when accessing the protected resources on a server, and that's why we're saying that a request is made on behalf of the user.

Let's see an example of an access token response in JSON format that a client may get from a successful authorization request:

```
{
  "access_token":"exampleAccessTokenValue",
  "expires_in":3600,
  "scope":"exampleScopeValue",
  "state":"exampleStateValue",
  "refresh_token":"exampleRefreshTokenValue"
}
```

The access token response contains the following fields/parameters:

- `access_token`: This is a mandatory parameter, defined by a string of characters, representing an authorization on behalf of the user who authorized the request, issued to the client application.

- `expires_in`: This is a mandatory parameter that tells the client application for how much time the issued token is valid. This numeric value is in seconds, so in our example this token is valid for one hour.

- `scope`: This is an optional parameter defining which parts (or types) of protected resources can be accessed on behalf of the user. More information on access scope is provided later in this chapter.

- `state`: This is an optional parameter, used by the client for its own purposes, most commonly for security checks. The state value that the client application sends during the request will be the same as the one it will receive as part of the access token response, so this parameter can be used for defending against man in the middle attacks.

- `refresh_token`: This parameter contains a string of characters that are to be used as a parameter when requesting a new token before its expiry. It is an optional parameter and some service providers don't use it.

Various other parameters may be included, too, and they are specific to the service providers that included them and serve some specific business logic. For example, some may return a `userId` parameter, representing some internal identifier for the user that has authorized the request.

One of the most important fields for a client application is `access_token`. This information is used when making the requests to protected resources. After that comes `expires_in` and `refresh_token`. Before the token expires, instead of going through the whole authorization flow, the client can get a new access token in a more transparent and simpler way by using the data from these fields. This way the user won't be bothered with authorization request dialogs again and again every time the access token expires.

It is important to store the `access_token` and the `refresh_token` in a secure way in the client application database, and it is a good practice to store and utilize properly all the fields that come with the access token response.

 The token response and other data that is exchanged in the OAuth 2.0 flow can be transferred in various data formats; the most commonly used formats are JSON and XML.

Refresh token

Access tokens should always expire; it's a rare case to have an access token that has an infinite lifetime, which is also considered a bad security practice. When a given access token used by the client has expired, the next time the client tries to use it to access some protected resources, it will get an error from the server.

The client uses the refresh token to get a new access token, by contacting the authorization server and supplying the data from the `refresh_token` field. If this data is valid, the authorization server returns a new access token response to the client.

Clients and endpoints

Let's recall the abstract flow diagram, step three: the client supplies the authorization grant to the authorization server in order to get an access token, but in order to do that the client also has to authenticate successfully.

For this to work, the client has to register with the authorization server. This registration is outside of the flow and is done separately. Also this registration is not defined in OAuth 2.0 and can be done in various ways. Most commonly the client developer registers the client on some web form and uses the data retrieved from there in order to do the authentication between the client and the authorization server, but more details on this is provided in the next chapter.

Client types and profiles

When registering the client, the authorization server has to know which type of client is being registered. There are two types:

- **Confidential client**: These type of client applications are capable of keeping the confidentiality of the credentials secure, for example, applications running on servers in secure/restricted environments
- **Public client**: These type of client applications are not capable of keeping the credentials secure, for example, pure JavaScript applications that run directly in the browser or mobile applications where the application logic is in a WebView

Additionally, clients are separated in three general profiles:

- **Web application**: This is considered to be a confidential client application, and it's meant to be a web application where data is stored securely on the server side of the application and cannot be accessed on the public/client side.
- **User-agent-based application**: This is an application that is first downloaded and then executed in a user-agent environment (for example, in a web browser). Since all data is downloaded, including credentials, this is a public application.
- **Native application**: This is also a public client. Applications that are installed on a device, which is used by the resource owner belong to this profile.

Endpoints

An endpoint is an HTTP URL string that defines the address which should be used in a certain request by an entity capable of making requests.

In OAuth 2.0 there are three important endpoints.

Two of them are server endpoints:

- **Authorization endpoint**: The client uses this endpoint in order to be authorized from the resource owner. If successful, the client obtains an authorization grant. There are exceptions to this behavior, like in the implicit grant flow, where the client obtains an access token from this endpoint.
- **Token endpoint**: The client uses this endpoint in order to supply the authorization grant and get an access token in return.

And one is a client endpoint:

- **Redirection (callback) endpoint**: The authorization server uses this endpoint in order to return data with authorization credentials to the client

The server endpoints are usually specified in the code of the client application, and the client endpoint is specified when registering the client with the authorization server.

In the next chapter we'll see practical examples of client registration.

Access scope

Scope is a parameter that can be used when a client makes a request to the authorization or token endpoints.

With this parameter the client can specify which parts (or types) of protected resources it wants to access on behalf of the owner. With scopes the client limits itself from all the resources that are available and this is a good security practice. When the request is processed, the authorization server validates the scope that is requested, and if it's invalid the client application won't get an access token. It is also very common for service providers to allow end users to review which scopes will be allowed upon granting the request.

Scope is an optional parameter and it's up to the implementation scenario what values it will have. There are some services such as the ones from Google that demand that scope is a mandatory parameter when making requests to their endpoints. Here, scope is used as a way to tell Google two things: which API services are requested and what is the degree of access requested for each one of them.

When developing a client application against a third party service to check which scopes are available, always search for developer documentation and guides supplied.

In services where scope is optional, if the client doesn't specify one, the OAuth 2.0 specification mandates that a default scope should be used. For every token there is always a scope in which it is set to operate, whether or not it was specified.

Summary

In this chapter, we have learned about key terms that are defined and used in OAuth 2.0, preparing ourselves to be able to understand with greater ease the following chapters, where the authorization flows are explained in detail.

In the next chapter, we will go through all the necessary steps that are common when developing a client application and we will go through the so called 'client registration' process.

3
First Step for Your Application

This chapter will help us to take the necessary steps that are common when developing a client application.

As mentioned, client applications can be web, mobile, desktop, or any other type, and use OAuth 2.0 for making requests to protected resources (files, data, or other services that an API may provide) on a given service provider, on behalf of the resource owner, most commonly the user.

OAuth 2.0 has significantly improved from OAuth 1.0 regarding this area — the focus of all the different types of applications and defining authorization flows for them.

Client registration

When developing an application that makes requests to protected resources on some service provider, and if this service uses OAuth 2.0 for authorization, then the first thing the client developer must do is to register the application at the given service provider.

Usually this happens on some web interface where the developer inserts the requested data, as name and website of the client application, uploads an image to serve as the application logo, and specifies the redirection (also called callback) endpoint.

To make it clearer, we'll go through several examples of client registration. First, let's see how it is done on Facebook. Let's go to the following URL after we log in to Facebook: `https://developers.facebook.com/apps`.

Select **Create New App**, as shown in the following screenshot:

We fill out the initial form and next we are greeted with more details and settings, as shown in the following screenshot:

What we see in the previous screenshot are the client ID and client secret, named **App ID** and **App Secret**.

Next, Facebook offers several accessible settings for different types of applications. For example, on the same page various options are given, as shown in the following screenshot:

In the case of choosing **Mobile Web**, the parameter named **Mobile Site URL** is actually the callback URL.

The callback URL is optional, and if the client doesn't override this endpoint with the `redirect_uri` parameter when making the authorization request, the one specified in the registration is used as default. This is the same for all service providers when registering and using OAuth 2.0. We'll cover this parameter in later chapters; for now it's good enough to be aware of the callback URL.

> When registering applications, after successfully filling out the data, every registration interface should provide the developer with the information that is needed to him or her, that is, the URL endpoints, unique client ID, and client secret for his/her application.

The client ID is used by the client application to identify itself when attempting to retrieve an access token. This information is public and anyone can find out a client ID for a given application, mostly because it's used as a parameter in the URL endpoints when making requests to the server.

On the other hand, the client secret is private information and it must remain confidential to the client application. If an application cannot keep this confidentiality (for example, pure JavaScript applications that run in the browser), then it is considered that it is a public client application and should omit this parameter when making requests to the server.

We can notice that the endpoints provided by Facebook are to be used over HTTPS. It is a must that the callback endpoint use HTTPS as well; the OAuth 2.0 specification requires the use of transport layer security. This means that **Transport Layer Security** (**TLS**) is used as a security mechanism and this way the tokens that are exchanged between the client application and the server are protected from interception.

Next, we'll explore one more example of client registration to realize that some services may require more information from the client developer and may offer some configuration parameters. This example in particular is **LinkedIn**, as shown in the following screenshot:

In the previous screenshot, the first two sections of the registration are shown, which require the client developer to enter roughly the same data as in the previous example with Facebook. Additionally, it's required that the developer enters a company name and names the purpose of the application. These fields have nothing to do with the OAuth 2.0 specification, but the service provider (in this case LinkedIn) decided that they are important and required.

The most interesting part of the registration is the following section:

As shown in the following screenshot, the client developer can define the default scope of the client application. With this the developer explicitly says which type of information and access the client application can be given by the service (in this case the LinkedIn API).

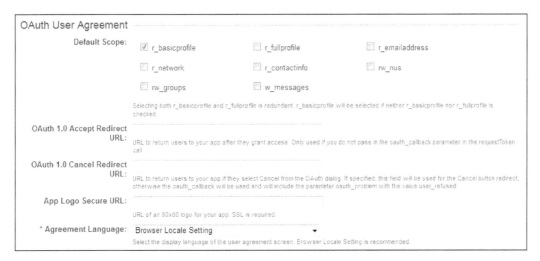

For example, if the application that the developer is making only needs to access the user's basic profile (to check out name, surname, and so on), then the developer would require only the r_basicprofile scope. If the application additionally needs to be able to access and send messages on behalf of the user, then the developer would tick the checkbox (in this case w_messages) for that scope too.

Defining the really needed scope is always recommended, instead of ticking all the boxes and marking all the scopes available as required.

 LinkedIn supports both OAuth 2.0 and OAuth 1.0; that's why there are some optional parameters that we are not filling in when registering. These are for legacy applications.

Now that we have set up an application on the service provider, and with that successfully registered the client, we can move on to the next step—implementing OAuth 2.0 in a particular type of application.

Summary

In this chapter, we went through the necessary steps that a client developer must go through before implementing one of the authorization flows, that is, registering the application on an authorization server. We went through two examples and learned which information authorization servers require, and which data is useful and needed by us, the client developers.

In the next chapter, we will see how OAuth 2.0 is used in web server applications, learn of the authorization code grant, which is used in that scenario, and go through a practical example.

4

OAuth for Web Server Applications

Have you ever signed into a website via Facebook, LinkedIn, or Google? For example, you're visiting a news website and you wanted to leave a comment on an article, and instead of creating an account there you just signed in by clicking on a button and choosing "Approve" in Facebook?

This is just one of the many examples where OAuth 2.0 is successfully and massively used, and this kind of flow — the redirecting between the website and Facebook and back — is based on the authorization code grant, probably the most frequently used OAuth 2.0 grant.

 In the OAuth 2.0 authorization framework specification (*RFC 6749*), this grant is defined in *Section 4.1*.

Authorization code grant

We can notice the following characteristics in the authorization code grant:

- The authorization code grant is used for confidential clients
- It uses redirection, so it is a redirection-based flow, between the client and the authorization service
- It requires the end user's approval for authorization, for example, by displaying a message in a web browser

 What is a confidential client? Refer to *Chapter 2, Terms You Need To Know*, where we covered the OAuth 2.0 terminology.

The authorization code grant is used to obtain access tokens and optionally refresh tokens. Access tokens are used to perform API requests on behalf of the user; refresh tokens are used to request new access tokens when needed and without the trouble to redo the whole grant flow and end user approval.

The following diagram shows a graphical representation of this flow, taken from the OAuth 2.0 specification:

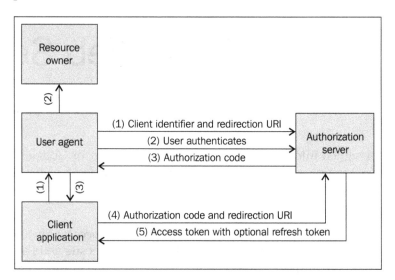

Let's go step-by-step and see how a client gets the authorization and retrieves an access token on behalf of the user:

1. First task is the initiation of the flow where the **Client application** is redirecting the **User agent** (for example, the browser) to the authorization endpoint.

2. Then the **Authorization server** authenticates the **Resource owner** (for example, you have to be logged into Facebook before you approve an authorization) and the owner chooses whether to authorize the request or not. Most commonly this happens in a browser window and this is the only step of the flow that is visible to the end user.

3. If the user authorizes the request, then he is redirected using the previously supplied redirection endpoint, from which the **Client application** gets the authorization code for that user.

4. Using this authorization code, the client makes a request for an access token on the specified server endpoint. Additionally, the client authenticates during the request and includes the redirection endpoint.

5. The **Authorization server** authenticates the client, validates the authorization code, and ensures that the redirection endpoints supplied in step 4 and 2 match each other. If valid, the **Authorization server** responds back with an access token (and optionally a refresh token). And when the **Client application** gets the access token, it can start making requests with it to some API on behalf of the user.

Basically, this flow can be divided into two parts, requesting authorization from the user and obtaining an authorization code, and once authorized requesting an access token with the authorization code. Next we'll see the authorization code grant in detail and see which parameters are used and which data is exchanged.

> It is common for the service providers that support OAuth 2.0 (the ones that host the resource servers) to have an internal page, similar to the application registration page that we discussed in the previous chapter, where end users, when logged in, can review which client applications they have given the authorization approval and revoke access if desired.

Requesting the authorization code

Requesting authorization is all about getting the user to authorize the client application and the authorization server to return an authorization code.

For this, first the client must be registered with the authorization server, and the client application will use the authorization endpoint specified in the registration details. This is covered in detail in *Chapter 3, First Step for Your Application*.

Making the request

The client application constructs the request address (that is, the request URL) from the endpoint and the parameters. For example, it may have the following form:

```
https://api.example-service.com/oauth/authorize?response_
type=code&client_id=CLIENT_ID_EXAMPLE&redirect_uri=REDIRECT_ENDPOINT_
EXAMPLE
```

There are several parameters that are part of the request URL, among which some are mandatory and some are optional. These parameters are explained as follows:

- `response_type`: This is a mandatory parameter and its value must be set to `code`.

- `client_id`: This is a mandatory parameter that is used for identification of the client application to the authorization server. The value is set with the data from the client registration with the authorization server.

- `redirect_uri`: This is an optional parameter, representing the endpoint to which the authorization server supplies the authorization code, if the authorization was approved by the end user.

- `scope`: This is an optional parameter that is used for specifying which parts (or types) of the protected resources are to be accessed on behalf of the owner.

- `state`: This is an optional parameter that can be used by the client for its own purposes, most commonly for security checks. When the authorization server redirects back to the `redirect_uri` parameter with the authorization code, it can additionally supply back the `state` parameter with the same value that was used in the request. This security precaution is strongly recommended for client developers.

The client redirects the end user to this endpoint, and the authorization server is validating the request and the user is asked for a decision, whether to allow the authorization request or not.

As shown in the following illustration, the user decision is displayed and conducted in a dialog message in the browser window, where it is specified which client application wants to be authorized and which privileges it requires (which are defined in the request parameter `scope`):

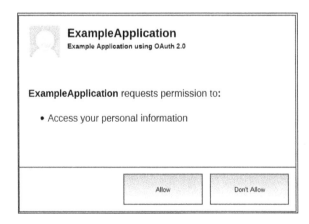

Lately, even some mobile applications use this flow (due to the fact that mobile operating systems provide mechanisms for secure storage), and display an embedded browser window in which the user logs in to the service provider and approves the authorization request.

After the user makes a decision, the authorization server redirects using the `redirect_uri` parameter. If this parameter was not supplied, the default redirect endpoint specified in the registration of the client application is used.

Successful authorization

If the user has approved the authorization, the server will do a redirect to the specified endpoint by the client, for example:

```
https://client.example.com/oauth/cb?code=AUTHORIZATION_
CODE&state=APP_STATE
```

From here the client application retrieves the authorization code from the `code` parameter. The second supplied parameter is `state` and it contains the same value that was specified in the request.

It is a security practice among authorization servers to expire authorization codes and not keep them for more than 10 minutes. So if the client application has retrieved the authorization code, it's advised to continue with the flow immediately and request an access token. If the code is expired the client application will have to go from the start of the flow again. Additionally, an authorization code can be used only once; we cannot get multiple different access tokens with the same authorization code.

Authorization error

If the user has denied the request or some other error has happened, such as missing parameter, invalid `client_id`, or a similar error, the client application will get an error response.

The client is redirected to the same redirect endpoint (or if this endpoint is invalid, then to the one specified in the client registration), for example:

```
https://client.example.com/oauth/cb?error=access_denied&state=APP_
STATE
```

The error parameter can contain one of the following values that can be helpful to the client developer to diagnose the problem:

- invalid_request: This value appears when there's a problem with the request, such as a missing parameter or value, a parameter included more than once, or a parameter with a malformed name.

- unauthorized_client: This value appears when the client application was not authorized.

- access_denied: This value appears when the end user (the resource owner) has denied the request.

- unsupported_response_type: This value appears when the authorization server cannot support the requested response. If in the request the response_type parameter is set to code, this error won't happen.

- invalid_scope: This value appears when the scope specified does not exist or is invalid.

- server_error: This value appears when an unknown error happens and the server cannot process the response. Very similar to HTTP 500 errors in web pages.

- temporarily_unavailable: This value appears when the authorization server cannot process the request at the given moment.

Besides the error parameter, few other parameters can be part of the response as well, such as:

- error_description: This is an optional parameter that may contain a message describing what the cause of the error was

- error_uri: This is an optional parameter containing a URI to a web document that should contain an additional description of the error

- state: This is a mandatory parameter that returns the exact value that was specified in the request with the same-named state parameter

 Proper handling of errors by the client application and friendly notifications to the end user are good development. The user will appreciate knowing what precisely is going on.

Requesting the access token

Once the client gets the authorization code, it can go on and request the access token. This is done between the client application and the server and requires no interaction from the end user.

Making the request

As with the authorization request, first the client constructs the request address from the specified endpoint and the parameters, resulting in the following example:

```
https://api.example-service.com/oauth/access_token?grant_
type=authorization_code&code=AUTHORIZATION_CODE&redirect_
uri=REDIRECT_EXAMPLE&client_id=ID_EXAMPLE
```

The request consists of the following parameters that are mandatory:

- `grant_type`: This parameter's value must be set to `authorization_code`.
- `code`: This is the authorization code previously retrieved from the authorization server.
- `redirect_uri`: This is the parameter where the authorization server should redirect the client and supply the access token. Additionally, if this parameter was used in the step where the authorization code was requested from the client, the values of `redirect_uri` in the authorization code request and this one must be the same.
- `client_id`: This parameter's value is set as per the data from the client registration with the authorization server, the same as in previous cases.

With the URL address prepared, the client application executes it by making an HTTP POST request, and the authorization server makes the following important checks:

- That the client is valid and already registered
- That the supplied authorization code is valid and not expired and belongs to the specified `client_id` parameter
- That the `redirect_uri` callback is the same as the one specified when the client requested the authorization code

Successful response

If all the checks are valid on the side of the authorization server, an access token and optionally a refresh token are created and sent as a response to the HTTP POST request.

The response body would contain a JSON (or XML) object and it may have the following form:

```
{
    "access_token":"exampleAccessTokenValue123",
    "expires_in":3600,
    "refresh_token":"exampleRefreshTokenValue123",
    "token_type":"Bearer"
}
```

The client application will have to process this response and store the values of the fields in a secure environment, especially access_token and refresh_token. After storing the data, the client can use it, for example by using access_token to authorize calls to some API methods in the service on behalf of the user.

Practical example

Now that we have covered the authorization code grant in detail it's time to do a practical example.

We will make an example web application that will use Dropbox as its authorization server and will implement the authorization code grant.

The web example application is based on Java technologies, namely, Spring MVC and JSP, and uses the Google GSON library for JSON parsing and Apache HTTP Client for making HTTP requests. The example is concise, elegant, and explained in detail so that developers familiar with other technologies should have no problem understanding it. When we open the root folder of the Example Application, important files that are part of it are as follows:

- src\main\webapp\WEB-INF\pages\home.jsp: This is the main page displayed when the Example Application is opened

- src\main\webapp\WEB-INF\pages\error.jsp: This is the page that we show when an error occurs

- src\main\java\example\authorization\MainController.java: This contains the Java logic of the Example Application.

Additionally, for added clarity we will check out cURL statements of the same HTTP requests that are performed in Java. cURL is a popular command line tool that is used for transferring data over various protocols, and it is often used as an HTTP client.

We will make an authorization request with Dropbox and, once the user has authorized the request, we will get the access token and then make a request to the Dropbox API in order to get the name of the user who authorized the request and display it.

First thing we have to do is to register the client application at Dropbox. Client registration is covered in *Chapter 3, First Step for Your Application*. In the case of Dropbox, registration is done on the following URL:

```
https://www.dropbox.com/developers/apps
```

The main entry point to the application for the user is the main.jsp page, consisting of HTML markup, where the important code is in the body tag:

```
<body>
    <p><a href="${authEndpoint}">Authorize</a></p>

    <p>Authentication code is: <span>${code}</span></p>

    <p>Access token is: <span>${accessToken}</span></p>

    <p>Your Dropbox username is: ${userName}.</p>
</body>
```

Downloading the example code

You can download the example code files for all Packt books you have purchased from your account at http://www.packtpub.com. If you purchased this book elsewhere, you can visit http://www.packtpub.com/support and register to have the files e-mailed directly to you.

The values for the authEndpoint, code, accessToken, and userName variables are separated, each in its own paragraph, and their values are supplied from the Spring Controller, which we'll analyze next. At this moment, let's see what these variables represent. These variables are explained as follows:

- The first paragraph contains the link for initiating authorization, where the href attribute specifies the endpoint to which the end user is redirected. The href attribute value is specified in the authEndpoint variable.

- In the second paragraph, the value of the authorization code is shown with the help of the code variable. This field will be empty when the client application is not authorized.

- The third paragraph contains the `accessToken` variable that shows the value of the access token. This field will be empty when the client application is not authorized.

- The last paragraph contains the `userName` variable that will show the name of the user of the authorized Dropbox account. This field will be empty when the client application is not authorized. When the client application has the access token, then it can make API requests to the server in order to retrieve the information.

Now let's switch to the `MainController` controller, in which the rest of the code is stored.

In it, first we define variables and their values for the endpoints and the client identifier and secret:

```
String authEndpoint =
    "https://www.dropbox.com/1/oauth2/authorize";
String tokenEndpoint = "https://api.dropbox.com/1/oauth2/token";
String accountInfoEndpoint =
    "https://api.dropbox.com/1/account/info";

String clientId = "insertValue";
String clientSecret = "insertValue";
String redirectURI = "http://localhost:8090/cb";
```

When the application is opened in the browser, the following controller handles the request:

```
@RequestMapping(value = "/", method = RequestMethod.GET)
public String mainPage(ModelMap model) {

    String authRequest = authEndpoint.concat("?response_type=code")
        .concat("&client_id=").concat(clientId)
        .concat("&redirect_uri=").concat(redirectURI)
        .concat("&state=1234");

    model.addAttribute("authEndpoint", authRequest);
    return "main";
}
```

We can see that it performs concatenations and builds the requested endpoint with the appropriate parameters. This value is put in the `model` parameter and, by doing this, it is accessible to be used as the `href` field in the HTML rendered in the browser. When the user clicks on the authenticate link, the end user will be redirected to the location.

The assigned `state` in the request is set to `1234`. This serves just as an example and in real world scenarios a securely random value should be generated and used.

The URL endpoint that is requested when the user clicks on authenticate, when represented as a CURL statement, has the following form:

```
curl -d response_type=code \
  -d client_id=insertValue \
  -d redirect_uri=http://localhost:8090/cb \
  -d state=1234
  https://www.dropbox.com/1/oauth2/authorize
```

Next, the user approves the authorization in Dropbox, and when redirected back the callback controller handles the request. Because we're running the Example Application on a local environment, we have set the callback/redirection endpoint to `http://localhost:8090/cb` in the `redirectURI` variable. The `localhost` parameter tells the browser that it should search for a locally hosted address; `8090` is the port on which the Example Application is running, and `/cb` is the handle we use for the redirection.

When the callback handler is requested by Dropbox's authorization server, the following code handles that:

```
@RequestMapping(value = "/cb", method = RequestMethod.GET)
public String callbackHandler(@RequestParam(value = "code", required =
true) String code,
    ModelMap model)
    throws IOException {
  //..
}
```

Note the use of the `@RequestParam` annotation, by which we instruct Spring Framework automatically to extract the value of the `code` parameter from the URL into a String. By doing the extraction we have the value of the authorization code available to us and we can use it in the method body.

Let's see what's going inside the method. First we add the value of the authorization code to the `model` parameter, in order to display it to the user.

```
model.addAttribute("code", code);
```

Next, we define the request URL in a series of concatenations of the endpoint variable and required parameters, resulting in the `tokenRequest` variable. We use this variable to perform a request for the access token, by defining a HTTP POST request with it and executing it with the help of the HTTP client.

```
String tokenRequest =
    tokenEndpoint
    .concat("?grant_type=authorization_code")
    .concat("&client_id=").concat(clientId)
    .concat("&client_secret=").concat(clientSecret)
    .concat("&redirect_uri=")
    .concat(URLEncoder.encode(redirectURI, "UTF-8"))
    .concat("&code=").concat(code);

HttpPost getAccessTokenRequest = new HttpPost(tokenRequest);
getAccessTokenRequest.addHeader("Accept", "application/json");

DefaultHttpClient httpClient = new DefaultHttpClient();
HttpResponse response = httpClient.execute(getAccessTokenRequest);
```

> We also specify a request header named accept, telling Dropbox that we expect a JSON as a response. Note that this is Dropbox specific, showing the nature of OAuth 2.0 where the implementation of the protocol may have additional customizations by the services that support it.

Next we create an HTTP client and execute this request, which when finished stores the result into the `HttpResponse` object.

This request, when represented as a CURL statement, has the following form:

```
curl -X POST \
  -d grant_type=authorization_code \
  -d client_id=insertValue \
  -d client_id=insertValue \
  -d redirect_uri=http://localhost:8090/cb \
  -d code=code
  https://www.dropbox.com/1/oauth2/token
```

If the response has a status code different from HTTP 200, it means that some error has occurred, so we display an error message to the user. The check is done using the following code:

```
if (response.getStatusLine().getStatusCode() != 200) {
  return handleError(response, model);
}
```

If it's an error we stop the flow and execute `handleError`, a custom method by which we show an error page to the user with a description.

```
private String handleError(HttpResponse response, ModelMap model) {
  model.addAttribute("errorMessage",
      "Error. HTTP status code: " +
        response.getStatusLine().getStatusCode()
    + "\nReason: " +
        response.getStatusLine().getReasonPhrase());

  return "error";
}
```

If it's an error, Spring Framework will return the `error.jsp` page; if it's not an error we continue. The content of the response is converted into an object called `AccessTokenResponse`, with the help of the GSON library, as shown in the following code:

```
final Gson gson = new Gson();
Reader streamReader = new
  InputStreamReader(response.getEntity().getContent());
AccessTokenResponse atResponse = gson.fromJson(streamReader,
  AccessTokenResponse.class);

model.addAttribute("accessToken", atResponse.access_token);
```

We define `AccessTokenResponse` inside `MainController`, as shown in the following code:

```
private static class AccessTokenResponse {
  String access_token;
  String token_type;
  String expires_in;
  String uid;
  // ..
}
```

And GSON will convert the data from the HTTP response we have provided into an instance of this custom class, by using the `fromJson` method.

Now that we have the access token, we can make requests to the Dropbox API with it on behalf of the user.

```
HttpGet getAccountInfoRequest = new HttpGet(accountInfoEndpoint);
getAccountInfoRequest.addHeader("Accept", "application/json");
getAccountInfoRequest.addHeader("Authorization", "Bearer " +
  atResponse.access_token);
response = httpClient.execute(getAccountInfoRequest);
```

With the "Accept" header we specify that JSON is expected as a response data format, and we add one more header named "Authorization". As a value of the authorization header we specify the access token and this way Dropbox will authorize the request and will know on behalf of which user it is made.

Again we make the check that the HTTP status of the response is not different from 200, and convert the response with GSON into a new object named `AccountInfoResponse`, as shown in the following code:

```
streamReader =
  new InputStreamReader(response.getEntity().getContent());
AccountInfoResponse aiResponse =
  gson.fromJson(streamReader, AccountInfoResponse.class);

model.addAttribute("userName", aiResponse.display_name);
```

We define `AccountInfoResponse` as well by using the following code:

```
private static class AccountInfoResponse {
  String display_name;
  String uid;
  // ..
}
```

To check the Dropbox's API, go to

```
https://www.dropbox.com/developers/core/docs#account-info
```

and see that there are more fields in the JSON response besides `display_name`, but we don't have to define them if we don't plan to use them.

By adding the value for `userName` to the `model` parameter everything planned for this example was done, so we finish it with the line

```
return "main";
```

where Spring Framework returns the `main.jsp` page to the user, with all the data we supplied in the `model` parameter.

In the end, after the user approves the authorization, the callback handler processes the response, gets the access token, and gets the account information from Dropbox. The client application may look like the following screenshot:

Summary

In this chapter, we have learned what web server applications are and how to use OAuth 2.0 in them by applying the authorization code grant. We have learned the authorization code grant in detail and did a practical code example by making a client application that uses Dropbox as an authorization and API server.

In the next chapter, we will learn what client side applications are, what implicit grants are, and how to use them in this type of applications. We will also create a practical code example, again using Dropbox as an authorization and API server.

5
OAuth for Client-side Applications

In the previous chapter, we learned how to use OAuth 2.0 in client web applications; applications that store their credentials and the access tokens on secure storage and keep them confidential.

As JavaScript grew more and more popular over the years, client-side applications rose as well. Applications that are mainly written in JavaScript and the code they contain is downloaded in the browser before its execution.

These applications may look and behave the same as traditional web server applications, but the fact that everything they need is first downloaded to the client (for example, the browser) makes them unable to keep some data confidential, if required.

Moreover, these types of applications are mostly created for the read-only scenarios and use cases. The reason is that the access token is public, and someone can obtain it and takes damaging actions on behalf of the user, such as modifying or deleting some of his data.

Implicit grant

OAuth 2.0 provides a grant flow specifically for client applications that are considered to be public clients (meaning unable to keep their credentials such as the client identifier and client secret in confidentiality) and it's called the implicit grant.

The main difference between the authorization code grant and implicit grant is that instead of using two requests—one for an authorization code and then another one for obtaining the access token with it—it makes one request and the client gets an access token as a result of the authorization request.

The characteristics of the implicit grant type are stated as follows:

- Used in public clients
- It's is a redirection-based flow (similar to the one in the authorization code grant)
- The access token is received as a parameter of the redirection endpoint upon successful completion of the request, similar to the authorization code parameter in the authorization request response in the authorization code grant

The following diagram shows a graphical representation of the flow, taken from the OAuth 2.0 specification:

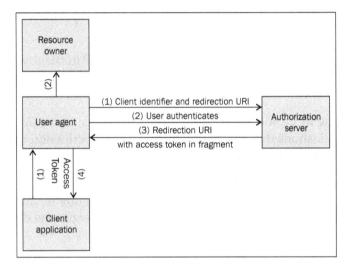

The flow consists of the following steps:

1. The first step is initiation of the flow. The client redirects the **User agent** to the **Authorization server** by using the authorization endpoint, the client identifier, and the redirection endpoint that will be used for the response.

2. The **Authorization server** authenticates the **Resource owner** and requests his decision whether to authorize or deny the request.

3. If the **Resource owner** authorizes the request (which is assumed), he is redirected back with response information, using the supplied redirection endpoint that was provided with the initial request. The response information is contained in the URL fragment that contains the access token and other parameters (we'll see the difference between a regular URL parameter and one found in a URL fragment in the detailed overview).

4. Now that the **User agent** (the browser) is redirected back, the access token included in the response is passed to the **Client application**.

Regarding revoking tokens, the resource owner (the end user) usually will be provided with some web interface by the service provider where, when logged in, he can list and review which client applications he has authorized and optionally revoke access if required. This is the same as in the case with the authorization code grant.

Requesting authorization

We'll assume that the client application is already registered with the authorization server, and the client developer gets the required data from the server, such as authorization endpoint and client identification.

The client application constructs the request, using the specified endpoint and the needed parameters and, for example, we may have the following form:

```
https://api.example-service.com/oauth/authorize?response_
type=token&client_id=CLIENT_ID_EXAMPLE&redirect_uri=REDIRECT_
ENDPOINT_EXAMPLE
```

The parameters that are used when constructing the request are as follows:

* `response_type`: This is a mandatory parameter, and its value must be set to `token`
* `client_id`: This is a mandatory parameter used for client identification
* `redirect_uri`: This is an optional parameter that represents the redirection endpoint used by the authorization server to return the access token if the authorization was approved by the user
* `scope`: This is an optional parameter
* `state`: This is an optional parameter

The `scope` and `state` parameters were discussed in *Chapter 04*, *OAuth for Web Server Applications*, so you can refer to that chapter if they aren't clear already.

With the request constructed, the client application redirects the end user to it. The authorization server checks whether all the parameters are valid. The end user is authenticated and is asked for a decision whether to allow the authorization request or not.

As in the authorization code grant, the user is asked for a decision whether to allow or deny the request.

Successful authorization

When the user approves the request, the server will do a redirect to the specified redirection endpoint and in response the access token will be contained as well.

For example, the response may have the following form:

```
https://client.example.com/oauth/cb#access_token=ACCESS_TOKEN_
VALUE&expires_in=3600
```

The first thing we notice is that the OAuth 2.0 related parameters are part of the fragment of the URL as they are after the hash (#) symbol. This is important to know because in the client application's code the developer may have to implement a different way of getting the values for the parameters.

URL fragments mean that all the parameters after the hash symbol are used only by the browser (that is used by the client-side (JavaScript) code that we have written and is executed in the browser) and these parameters are not sent to a server.

The parameters that can be included in the fragment are as follows:

- `access_token`: This is a mandatory parameter. Its value is the actual access token that the client application requires.
- `expires_in`: This is an optional and recommended parameter. It specifies the lifetime of the access token in seconds.
- `token_type`: This is a mandatory parameter as defined in the specifications, but in real life scenarios it can be found omitted from the response. Token type specifies what kind of a token is returned in the response and it may be utilized when implementing a client application against an authorization server with some additional security.
- `scope`: This is an optional parameter.
- `state`: This is a mandatory parameter in the response. If it was used when making the request, it will return the same value that was supplied then.

Another key difference compared to the authorization code grant is that, in an implicit grant, refresh tokens are not issued to the client application. When the access token expires the client has to initiate the whole implicit grant flow again.

 The OAuth 2.0 specification does not define how many characters long the access tokens should be.

Authorization error

If the request was denied by the user, or `redirect_uri` is missing or invalid, or `client_id` is missing or invalid, the client applications will get an error response from the server.

For example, the error response can be in the following form:

```
https://client.example.com/oauth/cb?error=access_denied&state=APP_
STATE
```

The parameters are the same as in the error response in the authorization code grant, but let's take a look at them again.

The most important is the `error` parameter, which can contain one of the following values, depending on what the cause of the error was:

- `invalid_request`: This error occurs when there's a problem with the request such as a missing parameter or value, a parameter included more than once, or a parameter with a malformed name.
- `unauthorized_client`: This error occurs when the client application was not authorized, or most probably the `client_id` parameter is invalid.
- `access_denied`: This error occurs when the end user (the resource owner) has denied the request.
- `unsupported_response_type`: This error occurs when the authorization server cannot support the requested response. If in the request the `response_type` parameter is set to `code`, this won't happen.
- `invalid_scope`: This error occurs when the scope specified does not exist or is invalid.
- `server_error`: This error occurs when an unknown error happened and the server cannot process the response. It is very similar to HTTP 500 errors in web pages.
- `temporarily_unavailable`: This error occurs when the authorization server cannot process the request at the given moment.

Additional parameters that the response may include are as follows:

- `error_description`: This is an optional parameter; it may contain a message describing what was the error cause
- `error_uri`: This is an optional parameter, containing a URI to a web document that should contain an additional description of the error
- `state`: This is a mandatory parameter that returns the exact value that was specified in the request with the same-named `state` parameter

Practical example

Now that we covered the implicit grant in detail we can create a practical example.

We will make an example web application that will use Dropbox as its authorization server and will implement the implicit grant.

The example application consists of an HTML page with JavaScript and jQuery where all the logic is coded. When this page is served from the server to the browser, everything including the `client_id` parameter is exposed to the public.

When we open the root folder of the example application, the important file is the following:

- `src\main\webapp\WEB-INF\pages\hello.jsp`: This contains the HTML template and the JavaScript logic

Additionally, for added clarity we will check out the cURL statements of the same HTTP requests that are performed in Java. cURL is a popular command line tool that is used for transferring data over various protocols, and it is often used as an HTTP client.

We will make an authorization request against Dropbox, and once the user has authorized the request with the access token we will make one more request to the Dropbox API and get the name of the user and display it.

First thing we have to do is to register the client application on Dropbox. These steps are covered in *Chapter 3*, *First Step for Your Application*. In the case of Dropbox, that can be done using the following URL:

`https://www.dropbox.com/developers/apps`.

The body of the HTML page is as follows:

```
<body>
    <p><a id="init-auth" href="">Authorize</a></p>
    <p id="auth-token-message">Client is not authorized!</p>
    <p id="auth-user-p">
        Your Dropbox username is: <span id="auth-user-message" >..</
span>.
    </p>
</body>
```

Here it's simple; we have three paragraph elements, as follows:

- The first paragraph element has an anchor element with the `init-auth` id. This will be the button the end user presses to authorize a request to Dropbox. The `href` attribute will contain the URI with the appropriate parameters to make the request valid and this is assigned from the JavaScript code we'll see next.

- In the second paragraph element, a message is shown that the user is not authenticated. When authorized, it will show the value of the access token.

- And in the third paragraph element, when the user has authorized the request, it will show his name.

Now let's take a look at the JavaScript code, which is embedded as part of the `head` tag.

The whole code is part of a function block:

```
$(function () {
    $("#auth-user-p").hide();
```

And the paragraph that will show the authorized user is hidden with the jQuery `hide` function.

Next we define three variables:

- `clientId`: This variable will contain the client ID acquired from the Dropbox registration

- `AuthEndpoint`: This variable will be used as an authorization endpoint

- `APIEndpoint`: This variable will be used to call methods from the Dropbox API after getting an access token

```
var clientId = "CLIENT_ID";
var AuthEndpoint = "https://www.dropbox.com/1/oauth2/
authorize";
var APIEndpoint = "https://api.dropbox.com";
```

Next in the `AuthenticationURL` variable the parameters are added to the authorization endpoint with the appropriate values, and with this we have constructed the URL for the request and added the jQuery's `attr` function to the `init-auth` link.

With this, when the user clicks on the **Authorize** button, the flow will start.

```
var AuthenticationURL = AuthEndpoint +
        "?response_type=token" +
        "&client_id=" + clientId +
        "&redirect_uri=" + window.location +
        "&state=XXXYYYY";
$("#init-auth").attr("href", AuthenticationURL);
```

 The assigned `state` parameter in the request is set to "XXXYYYY". This serves just as an example; in real world scenarios a securely random value should be generated and used.

This URL endpoint that is requested when the user clicks on **Authorize** has the following form, when represented as a CURL statement:

```
curl -d response_type=token \
  -d client_id=insertValue \
  -d redirect_uri=http://localhost:8090/ \
  -d state=XXXYYYY \
  https://www.dropbox.com/1/oauth2/authorize
```

The next of the code checks whether the user has chosen whether to authorize the request or not (after Dropbox has redirected back to our client application), and uses the information from the response.

If the value in `document.location.hash` is not empty, that means that there is a response in the fragment section (the data after the hash character in the URL) and by making this check we know whether the page is loaded by a redirection.

```
if (document.location.hash !== "") {
```

If the check returns a true value, then this is a redirection with some data in the URL fragment. This means that we can proceed. We can extract the access token with a regular expression using the following code:

```
var token = decodeURI(
        (RegExp('access_token=' + '(.+?)(&|$)').exec(document.
location.hash)||[,null])[1]
        );
```

For the sake of not going off-topic, we will not dwell into the details of how the regular expression works.

Next we change the text in the paragraphs, letting the user know that the client application has returned from the authorization request.

```
$('#init-auth').text("Authorize again");
$('#auth-token-message').text("Your token is: " + token);
```

And finally, with the use of the access token, we make an AJAX request with the help of jQuery and ask Dropbox's API to give us the user information on behalf of the user, whose access token we have obtained.

Notice how we use `xhr.setRequestHeader` to put in an authorization header and use the token as its value. Without this, the Dropbox server will not know who is making the request and we will not be able to get the data from the API.

When the request is finished, we get a response showing who the user is on the page.

```
$.ajax({
    url: APIEndpoint + '/1/account/info',
    beforeSend: function (xhr) {
        xhr.setRequestHeader('Authorization',
        "Bearer " + token);
        xhr.setRequestHeader('Accept',
        "application/json");
    },
    success: function (response) {
        $('#auth-user-p').show();
        if (response) {
            $("#auth-user-message")
            .text(response.display_name);
        } else {
            $('#auth-user-p').text("An error occurred!");
        }
    }
});
    }
});
```

In the end, after a successful authorization and redirection back to the client application, the client application may look like the following screenshot:

Summary

In this chapter, we have learned what client-side applications are and how to use OAuth 2.0 in them by applying the implicit grant flow. We have learned the implicit grant in detail, and after that we did a practical example by making a client application that uses Dropbox as an authorization and API server.

In the next chapter, we will learn how to use OAuth 2.0 in mobile applications, check out which OAuth grants can be used and how, and look at some examples.

6
OAuth for Mobile Applications

In the previous chapters, we learned how to use OAuth 2.0 in the client-side applications, such as public clients that are unable to keep the client identifier and client secret confidential, and in web applications that are considered confidential clients. In the first case we used the authorization code grant flow and in the second case the implicit grant flow is used.

Now, as we move on to the mobile client applications, we may ask ourselves which OAuth 2.0 grant flow should be used. The answer is that both authorization code grant and implicit grant are suitable, and depending on the security environment the proper one is to be chosen. If the mobile operating system provides methods for secure storage, then the authorization code grant can be used; if not, the implicit grant can be used.

In this chapter we'll see how client applications for Android and iOS can use these grants. If the target/favorite mobile platform is not one of these two, you need not worry as the principles and advice mentioned in this chapter are applicable to every modern mobile operating system.

Custom URL scheme

Let's suppose that we are registering the application on the authorization server to get the needed details such as client_id in order to implement a successful flow. Registration is covered in detail in *Chapter 3*, *First Step for Your Application* with one difference: the callback endpoint (also known as the redirect_uri parameter) is not the same.

In both authorization code and implicit grants, the callback endpoint is the URL to which the authorization server redirects back and returns the information to the client application.

Here, first we have to register a custom URL scheme with the client application, a scheme that will be applicable on an operating system level, enabling us to forward all redirects to our client application.

For example, we may specify that the `redirect_uri` parameter will have the following form:

```
app123://cb
```

This will replace, for example, the following one: `https://client.example.com/cb`. This also means that the `app123` scheme is in use, the scheme is the first part of the URL.

Every time a URL that uses this scheme is opened, our client application will be launched to handle it and, when the authorization server redirects back to the client with the authorization response, the client application will handle that as well.

 If the mobile operating system provides no support for the custom URL schemes, or we don't want to use them for some reason, a conventional redirect URI can be used, as long as the application has access to the addresses being requested in the user agent.

Android

To register a custom URL scheme in Android, all we have to do is edit the `AndroidManifest.xml` file and include the following code in the appropriate activity block:

```xml
<intent-filter>
    <data android:scheme="app123" />
    <action android:name="android.intent.action.VIEW" />
    <category android:name="android.intent.category.DEFAULT" />
    <category android:name="android.intent.category.BROWSABLE" />
</intent-filter>
```

And when handling the event, use the following code:

```java
Uri data = getIntent().getData();
if (data != null) {
  // handler logic
}
```

iOS

Registration of a custom URL scheme in iOS is somewhat similar to Android but instead of a textual editor we use a graphical editor. We open the application's-`info.plist` file from the XCode project navigator, and it will show a table with the following columns: `Key`, `Type`, and `Value`.

Next, we expand the row with the `URL Types` key; it will show an `Item 0` field, and we add two new rows inside it with the following keys:

- **URL identifier**: This will have some values that will be a unique string, for example `com.packtpublishing.oauth.mobile`
- **URL schemes**: This will be an array and will have one string item, which will have the `app123` value

Or if we open this file with a textual editor, the content of this configuration will look like the following code:

```
<key>CFBundleURLTypes</key>
    <array>
        <dict>
            <key>CFBundleURLName</key>
            <string>com.packtpublishing.oauth.mobile</string>
        </dict>
        <dict>
            <key>CFBundleURLSchemes</key>
            <array>
                <string>app123</string>
            </array>
        </dict>
    </array>
```

And that's it! To handle this event in iOS we implement the following method:

```
- (BOOL)application:(UIApplication *)application
handleOpenURL:(NSURL *)url {
  // handler logic
}
```

Implicit grant example

For illustration, we will look at an example with the implicit grant. We are not going to cover it in detail as we can refer to the previous chapter. We'll just go through the important information that we will require while using it in mobile applications.

The implementation will be very similar to the one in the client-side applications, with two differences: the first difference will be that instead of clicking on a link in the client-side web, that will be done inside the mobile application; and the second difference is that if we are using a custom URL scheme, it is a different `redirect_uri`.

Requesting authorization

The client application constructs the request, using the specified endpoint and the needed parameters, and for example we may have the following form:

```
https://api.example-service.com/oauth/authorize?response_
type=token&client_id=CLIENT_ID_EXAMPLE&redirect_uri=app123%3A%2F%2Fcb
```

> When constructing HTTP requests (not only in OAuth 2.0) we need to encode the strings before assigning them as values for the parameters so that the request will be valid and not misinterpreted. That's why when encoding the `app123://cb` character string as a value for the `redirect_uri` parameter, it becomes `app123%3A%2F%2Fcb`. URL encoding and decoding is pretty simple and there are numerous online tools as well as support in programming language libraries for that.

Successful authorization

If the authorization was successful, meaning there were no errors, the `client_id` parameter was valid, and in the end the user has approved the authorization, the authorization server will redirect the client to the `redirect_uri` parameter and the response may have the following form:

```
app123://cb#access_token=ACCESS_TOKEN_VALUE&expires_in=3600
```

Authorization error

And if any error occurred, or the user denied the authorization request, the response may have the following form:

```
app123://cb#error=ERROR_VALUE&state=APP_STATE
```

> If the client gets an error, it's a good practice to show the user a friendly message that there was an error and to ask him whether he would like to try authorizing the client again.

Summary

In this chapter, we have learned how to use OAuth 2.0 in mobile applications by applying the authorization code grant and the implicit grant. We learned about custom URL schemes and how to use them in Android and iOS, and we learned how to make the authorization request with this custom scheme.

In the next chapter, we will learn what trusted applications are, will learn about the Resource Owner Password Credentials grant and the client credentials grant, and will make a practical example of these two new grant types for this type of application.

7
OAuth for Trusted Applications

In the previous chapter, we learned how to use OAuth 2.0 in mobile applications. We also learned about custom URL schemes, how to define them and how to use them. Up to this point in this book, we have covered the authorization code grant and the implicit grant, two out of the four grants defined in the OAuth 2.0 specification.

In this chapter, we will cover the remaining two grants defined in the OAuth 2.0 specification—the Resource Owner Password Credentials grant (which we can call the password grant for short) and the client credentials grant.

These two grants are most suitable in environments where trust and information confidentiality are assured. For example, the password grant can be used in internal environments and in scenarios where the authorization server and the client application(s) are by the same creator; and the client credentials grant is mostly used in cases when the client application wants to access some service API on behalf of itself and not on behalf of the user. Because of the fact that these two grants are suitable for less use cases and scenarios compared to the authorization code grant and the client credentials grant, they are supported by fewer service providers.

Note that the authorization code grant is used in trusted client applications as well, but used for those client applications that want to request a token on behalf of a resource owner (a user), or are able to utilize the web redirection flow instead of explicitly requiring the username and password to be entered.

Resource owner password credentials grant

The password grant is a grant flow where the client application, together with its client identifier and secret, sends the user's username and password in exchange for an access token. Instead of the user having to log in and approve the authorization request in some web interface — as in the authorization code grant — here the user may enter his username and password in the client application UI directly.

Additionally, this flow is good for client applications that are migrating to OAuth 2.0 and previously used some other form of API authentication, most commonly HTTP Basic or Digest. From the user's perspective, the client application may look and behave the same, but instead of transmitting the username and password to authenticate every request made to the API, it will do that only once in the beginning in order to obtain the access token.

Key characteristics of the password grant type are as follows:

- Used in confidential clients
- Uses the username and password of the resource owner
- The flow is not redirection-based; it takes only a request from the client application to the authorization server, and the user is not being redirected between interfaces to authorize the request

 In the OAuth 2.0 Authorization Framework specifications (RFC 6749), the Resource Owner Password Credentials grant is defined in section 4.3.

Let's take a look at a graphical representation of the flow, shown in the following diagram, taken from the OAuth 2.0 specification:

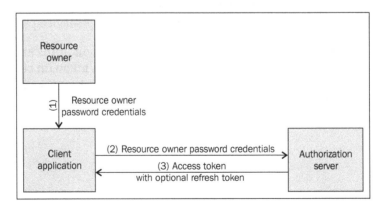

The flow consists of the following steps:

1. The resource owner (for example, the user) supplies the Client application with his username and password.

2. The client application makes a request to the Authorization server, including the user's credentials and also his own identifier and secret.

3. The Authorization server authenticates the client based on his identifier and secret, checks whether it is authorized for making this request, and checks the resource owner credentials and other parameters supplied. If all checks pass successfully, the Authorization server returns an access token in response.

> As a security precaution, it is highly advised that the client application, once it gets the access token, discards and does not store the username and password that the user has entered.

Requesting authorization

We'll assume that the client application is already registered with the authorization server, a step described in *Chapter 3*, *First Step for Your Application*.

The client application constructs the request address using the specified endpoint and the parameters, for example, `https://api.example-service.com/oauth/authorize?grant_type=password&client_id=CLIENT_ID_EXAMPLE&client_secret=CLIENT_SECRET&username=USERNAME&password=PASSWORD`.

When constructed, the address is being executed as an HTTP POST request, and if successful the client application will get an access token in return as part of the response body.

The parameters that are used when constructing the request are the following:

*   `grant_type`: This is a mandatory parameter, always set to `password`
*   `username`: This is a mandatory parameter supplied by the resource owner (the user)
*   `password`: This is a mandatory parameter supplied by the resource owner (the user)
*   `client_id`: This is an optional parameter used for client identification
*   `client_secret`: This is an optional parameter used for client identification
*   `scope`: This is an optional parameter, as in all previous cases, used for specifying which parts (or types) of protected resources can be accessed on behalf of the owner

Note that the authentication method between the client application and the authorization server may vary, and this is why the client identifier and secret are specified as optional. But in most of the cases they are part of the request URL. Sometimes, some custom additional parameters may have to be included as well, so always refer to the developer documentation supplied for the given service for which the client application is developed.

 How the client application asks for the user credentials and obtains them is out of the scope of the OAuth 2.0 specification. A common practice is for the client application to display a dialog box to the user asking him to enter this information.

Successful authorization

When the authorization server handles the request from the client, several validations are in place, such as follows:

- Validation of the client identification and secret, additionally assuring that the client is authorized to make the request
- Validation of the credentials of the resource owner

If the validations pass successfully, the authorization server will make a response with an access token and optionally with a refresh token.

In the body of the response, a JSON (or XML or other) object will be included representing the response. An example is shown as follows:

```
{
    "access_token":"exampleAccessTokenValue123",
    "token_type":"example",
    "expires_in":3600,
    "refresh_token":"exampleRefreshTokenValue123"
}
```

The fields that are part of the response are:

- `access_token`: This is a mandatory parameter and its value is the actual access token the client application may store and use later
- `token_type`: This is a mandatory parameter, a string representing what kind of a token is the one returned in the response
- `expires_in`: This is an optional and recommended parameter that specifies the lifetime of the access token in seconds

- `refresh_token`: This is an optional parameter used by the client to renew an access token whose lifetime has expired

> In some OAuth implementations of the authorization server, some other additional parameters may be included in the response as well. This is usually done to provide some additional business logic.

Authorization error

If the authorization request failed for any reason, the authorization server may return a response containing information regarding the error. Again, this may be in JSON format (or XML or other) and may have the following format:

```
{
  "error":"invalid_request",
  "error_description":"Username parameter missing",
  "error_uri": https://example-service.com/docs/oauth/
}
```

The `error` parameter can contain one of the several values listed as follows, describing the nature of the problem that has occurred:

- `invalid_request`: The `error` parameter contains this value when there's a problem with the request, either a missing parameter or value, a parameter included multiple times or missing, or a parameter with a malformed name.

- `invalid_client`: The `error` parameter contains this value when the authentication of the client fails. This can happen if authentication parameters are missing (the client identifier and secret) or if the client tries to authenticate with an unsupported method.

- `invalid_grant`: The `error` parameter contains this value when the grant specified is invalid, expired, or revoked, or it was issued to another client. For example, some services don't allow requesting a new access token until the one already issued is not expired.

- `unauthorized_client`: The `error` parameter contains this value when the client was authenticated by the authorization server, but has no authorization to use the grant requested.

- `unsupported_grant_type`: The `error` parameter contains this value when the grant that was requested is not supported by the authorization server.

- `invalid_scope`: The `error` parameter contains this value when the scope specified in the request was not valid, unknown, or malformed. In these situations check the developer documentation by the service provider to see which scopes are available and which ones can be used.

Additionally, the optional parameter `error_description` may contain a short message explaining the error, and the optional parameter `error_uri` may contain a link to a web document containing a more detailed explanation. Only the `error parameter` is mandatory.

Client credentials grant

The client credentials grant provides a specific grant flow in which the resource owner (that is, the user) is not involved.

In this grant, the client application requests an access token only with his own credentials (the identifier and secret) and uses the access token on behalf of the client application itself. In contrast, previously we used the access token on behalf of the user who authorized the request.

This grant flow is good when a service provider wants to provide some API methods that are to be used by the client application in general, instead of methods that apply to a certain resource owner, for example, API methods for statistics, maintenance, or something similar. This way of using an API is also referred to as Userless access.

Key characteristics of the client credentials grant type:

- Used by confidential clients
- The flow is not redirection-based
- Useful in scenarios where the client application communicates directly with the service provider and not on behalf of a resource owner
- The resource owner is not part of the flow

In the OAuth 2.0 Authorization Framework specification (RFC 6749), the client credentials grant is defined in section 4.4.

Let's take a look at a graphical representation of the flow, shown in the following diagram, taken from the OAuth 2.0 specification:

The flow consists of the following steps:

1. The Client application makes a request to the Authorization server and performs authentication.

2. The Authorization server authenticates the client based on his identifier and secret and makes a response. If the client is authenticated and the parameters supplied are valid, the client gets an access token as a response.

Requesting authorization

As before, we assume that the client application is already registered with the authorization server.

The client application constructs the request address, using the specified endpoint and the parameters, for example, `https://api.example-service.com/oauth/authorize?grant_type=client_credentials&client_id=CLIENT_ID_EXAMPLE&client_secret=CLIENT_SECRET`.

When constructed, the address is being executed as an HTTP POST request and if successful, the client application will get an access token in return as part of the response body. It's pretty much the same as in the password grant, but with fewer parameters.

The parameters that are used when constructing the request are the following:

- `grant_type`: This is a mandatory parameter, always set to `client_credentials`

- `scope`: This is an optional parameter, as in all previous cases used for specifying which parts (or types) of protected resources are to be accessed on behalf of the owner

- `client_id`: This is an optional parameter used for client identification

- `client_secret`: This is an optional parameter used for client identification

Client identifier and secret are specified as optional, due to the fact that the authentication method between the client application and the authorization server may vary, but in most of the cases they are a part of the request URL.

Successful authorization

If the client is authenticated and the supplied fields are successfully validated, the authorization server will respond with an access token.

The body of the response may have the following format:

```
{
  "access_token":"exampleAccessTokenValue123",
  "token_type":"example",
  "expires_in":3600
}
```

Very important to note is that the client credentials grant is not issuing a refresh token. All other fields in the response are the same as in password grant and authorization code grant:

- `access_token`: This is a mandatory parameter; its value is the actual access token the client application may store and use later

- `token_type`: This is a mandatory parameter, a string representing what kind of a token the one returned in the response is

- `expires_in`: This is an optional and recommended parameter that specifies the lifetime of the access token in seconds

Authorization error

The error response is the same as the one in the password grant discussed previously in this chapter; we can look there for additional information when an error occurs.

Practical example

Now we will work out a practical example for both grants covered in this chapter.

Due to the fact that these two grants are less popular and are suitable for less use cases and scenarios, compared to the authorization code grant and the client credentials grant, they can be found in fewer cases.

One of the service providers that uses OAuth 2.0 for authorization of its API and supports these two grants is **Zendesk**, a cloud-based customer service software solution. Among other services, they also offer an API on which client applications can be made and have implemented all four grants defined in the OAuth 2.0 specification.

We will create an example web application that will use Zendesk as its authorization server. It will contain implementations of both password grant flow and client credentials grant flow, and when executed it will request two tokens, one by using each grant. When opened in the browser, it will display the values of both access tokens.

It will be based on the same Java technologies as the example application for the authorization code grant: Spring MVC and JSP as the main components, Google GSON library for JSON parsing, and Apache HTTP client for making HTTP requests. As with the previous examples, this one is also concise, elegant, and explained in detail so that developers familiar with other technologies should have no problem understanding it.

When we open the root folder of the example application, the important files that are a part of it are the following:

- `src\main\webapp\WEB-INF\pages\home.jsp`: This is the main page displayed when the example application is opened
- `src\main\webapp\WEB-INF\pages\error.jsp`: This is the page that we show when an error occurs
- `src\main\java\example\password\MainController.java`: This file contains the Java logic of this example application, for both grants

 The example application can be downloaded from `http://www.packtpub.com`, containing all the files and instructions on how to compile and start them.

Additionally, for added clarity we will check out cURL statements of the same HTTP requests that are performed in Java. cURL is a popular command line tool that is used for transferring data over various protocols, and it is often used as an HTTP client.

Moving on, first thing we have to do is register a client application at Zendesk. For this purpose we will create a trial account, and register the client application at the following URL (where `user_id` is replaced with the one that was chosen when creating the account, also referred to as `subdomain`):

`https://USER_ID.zendesk.com/settings/api#oauth_clients`

For more information on this process, client registration is covered in *Chapter 3, First Step for Your Application.*

Let's start with the code. The main entry point of the application for the user is the `main.jsp` page, consisting of HTML markup, where the important code is in the body tag:

```
<body>
    <p>Access token from Password Grant flow is:
      <span>${accessTokenPWGrant}</span>
    </p>
    <p>Access token from Client Credentials Grant flow is:
      <span>${accessTokenCCGrant}</span>
    </p>
</body>
```

The values for the variables `accessTokenPWGrant` and `accessTokenCCGrant` are separated in their respective paragraphs, and their values are supplied from the spring controller that we'll analyze next. At this moment, let's see what they represent:

- The variable `accessTokenPWGrant` will show the value of the retrieved access token by using the password grant flow
- The variable `accessTokenCCGrant` will show the value of the retrieved access token by using the client credentials grant flow

The rest of the code resides in the `MainController` Java class. First, we define the needed variables and their values in it:

```
String clientId = "insertValue";   // client identifier
String clientSecret = "insertValue";   // client secret
String user_id = "insertValue";     // user/organization id
String username = "insertValue";   // account log-in email
String password = "insertValue";   // account log-in password
```

 We update the values of these variables with real ones in order that the example works properly. The same goes for the cURL statement examples.

The only endpoint defined is the one used for requesting the token:

```
String tokenEndpoint =
  "https://" + user_id +".zendesk.com/oauth/tokens";
```

Notice that we don't need to specify authorization and redirect/callback endpoints; these two flows don't need them.

Next, we define a class named `AccessTokenResponse` that will be used by GSON to convert the response from the request for access token into an instance of this class, providing a far easier way to use the response data:

```
private static class AccessTokenResponse {
  String access_token;
  String token_type;
  String expires_in;
  String scope;
  String refresh_token;
  // ..
}
```

All the fields that may be part of the response are specified. If they don't exist in the actual response from the server they will be `null` when the object is created by GSON. We can also add additional custom fields, if there are any.

When the application is opened in the browser, the following code handles the request:

```
@RequestMapping(value = "/", method = RequestMethod.GET)
public String mainPage(ModelMap model)
  throws IOException {

  model.addAttribute("accessTokenPWGrant",
    getATWithPasswordGrantFlow().access_token);
  model.addAttribute("accessTokenCCGrant",
    getATWithClientCredentialsGrantFlow().access_token);
  return "main";
}
```

We're using Spring's `@RequestMapping` annotation to map the main URL / to the `mainPage` handler method. Because this page is opened in a browser, it's mapped to the HTTP GET request method.

Inside the `mainPage` handler method, we get an instance of the `AccessTokenResponse` two times, for both flows, the first time by executing the `getATWithPasswordGrantFlow` method and the second time by executing the `getATWithClientCredentialsGrantFlow` method.

For both methods, once we get the `AccessTokenResponse` we get the value of the `access_token` field and put it in `model`. The first time it is put in as a value for the variable named `accessTokenPWGrant` and the second for the one named `accessTokenCCGrant`. By putting them in `model`, they are accessible to be used and displayed in HTML, which is rendered and served to the browser.

The next step is to define the code in these two methods by implementing the flows so that in the end they will return an access token response.

Resource owner password credentials grant

When we call the `getATWithPasswordGrantFlow` method in `mainPage`, we execute the whole password grant flow inside it and as a response of that method we get an instance of `AccessTokenResponse`:

```
model.addAttribute("accessTokenPWGrant",
  getATWithPasswordGrantFlow().access_token);
```

Let's see this method in detail:

```
private AccessTokenResponse getATWithPasswordGrantFlow()
    throws IOException {

  String tokenRequest =
    tokenEndpoint.concat("?grant_type=password")
      .concat("&client_id=").concat(clientId)
      .concat("&client_secret=").concat(clientSecret)
      .concat("&username=")
      .concat(URLEncoder.encode(username, "UTF-8"))
      .concat("&password=")
      .concat(URLEncoder.encode(password, "UTF-8"));

  HttpPost getAccessTokenRequest =
    new HttpPost(tokenRequest);
  getAccessTokenRequest.addHeader(
    "Accept",
    "application/json");

  DefaultHttpClient httpClient =
    new DefaultHttpClient();
  HttpResponse response =
    httpClient.execute(getAccessTokenRequest);

  if (response.getStatusLine().getStatusCode() != 200) {
    printError(response);
    return null;
  }

  final Gson gson = new Gson();
  Reader streamReader =
    new InputStreamReader(
```

```
        response.getEntity().getContent());
    AccessTokenResponse atResponse =
      gson.fromJson(
        streamReader,
        AccessTokenResponse.class);

    return atResponse;
  }
```

We can see that it consists of several parts:

1. First, we define the request URL in a series of concatenations of the token endpoint variable and the required parameters and their values, resulting in `tokenRequest`. During that process for some values that are concatenated, we use `URLEncoder.encode` in order to make sure that all characters are encoded properly (such as special characters in a password).

2. Next, with this token request URL, we create an HTTP POST request object and add a request header to it named `Accept` with value `application/json`, telling Zendesk that we expect a JSON format as a response.

3. Now that the `HttpPost` request object is created, we create an HTTP client and execute it. We store the result of the execution in an `HttpResponse` object, named `response`.

4. Next, we check the response. If the response has an HTTP status code different than `200`, then it means that an error occurred, so we print the reason in console and exit the method by returning `null`. If there's no error, then we move on.

5. We create a GSON object so that we are able to use it, then we read the body of the response into a `streamReader`, and finally call `gson.fromJson` to deserialize the data into an instance of `AccessTokenResponse`.

6. In the end, we make a return statement, supplying the access token response.

The HTTP request that is constructed and executed in the previous steps, when represented as a cURL statement has the following form:

```
curl -X POST \
  -H "Accept: application/json" \
  -d "grant_type=password" \
  -d "client_id=insertValue" \
  -d "client_secret=insertValue" \
  -d "username=insertValue" \
  -d "password=insertValue" \
  https://USER_ID.zendesk.com/oauth/tokens
```

If we run the client application, it may look like the following screenshot:

Here, the access token was successfully obtained with the use of the password grant, and its value is displayed on the page.

Next, we'll get the second access token, utilizing the client credentials grant flow, as shown in the screenshot in the following section.

Client credentials grant

As with the previous grant, here we proceed in the same fashion: we call the `getATWithClientCredentialsGrantFlow` method in `mainPage`, we execute the whole client credentials grant flow inside it, and we get an instance of `AccessTokenResponse` as a response.

```
model.addAttribute("accessTokenCCGrant",
  getATWithClientCredentialsGrantFlow().access_token);
```

Let's see this method in detail:

```
private AccessTokenResponse getATWithClientCredentialsGrantFlow()
  throws IOException {

  String tokenRequest =
    tokenEndpoint
      .concat("?grant_type=client_credentials")
      .concat("&client_id=").concat(clientId)
      .concat("&client_secret=").concat(clientSecret)
      .concat("&user_id=").concat(user_id);
```

```java
HttpPost getAccessTokenRequest =
  new HttpPost(tokenRequest);
getAccessTokenRequest.addHeader(
  "Accept",
  "application/json");

DefaultHttpClient httpClient =
  new DefaultHttpClient();
HttpResponse response =
  httpClient.execute(getAccessTokenRequest);

if (response.getStatusLine().getStatusCode() != 200) {
  printError(response);
  return null;
}

final Gson gson = new Gson();
Reader streamReader =
  new InputStreamReader(
    response.getEntity().getContent());
AccessTokenResponse atResponse =
  gson.fromJson(
    streamReader,
    AccessTokenResponse.class);

return atResponse;
}
```

There are two differences in the code compared to the previous grant. The first difference is in the parameters that are a part of the request URL. In the password grant flow we had the following parameters: client_id, client_secret, username, and password. In this flow, for client credentials, we have the following parameters: client_id, client_secret, and user_id. The second difference is also in the parameters: in the password grant flow we set the value of the grant_type parameter to password, and in the client credentials grant flow we set it to client_credentials.

The parameter user_id is a custom one from Zendesk, and it is not part of the OAuth 2.0 specification. This is just another example showing us that implementations of various OAuth 2.0 flows may vary and they are not identical between service providers. And this is why we are always encouraged to read the developer documentation provided by the service for which we're developing a client application.

The HTTP request that is constructed and executed in the previous steps, when represented as a cURL statement, has the following form:

```
curl -X POST \
   -H "Accept: application/json" \
   -d "grant_type=password" \
   -d "client_id=insertValue" \
   -d "client_secret=insertValue" \
   -d "user_id=USER_ID " \
   https://USER_ID.zendesk.com/oauth/tokens
```

In the end, if we run the client application, it may look like the following screenshot:

The client application successfully shows the values of the obtained access tokens for both grant flows that we have learned about.

Summary

In this chapter, we have learned which are trusted and first-party applications and learned about the Resource Owner Password Credentials grant and the client credentials grant. We learned how to perform authorization requests for these grants and saw code examples for them as well.

In the next chapter, we will dive into security considerations. We'll learn about the most common threats and their countermeasures, for all grant flows that we have learned so far and that are a part of the OAuth 2.0 specification.

8
Security Considerations

In the previous chapter we learned about the Resource Owner Password Credentials grant and the client credentials grant, and with that we covered all OAuth 2.0 grants that are defined in the OAuth 2.0 specification.

Given that information security is of paramount importance, it is important to know what data we transmit over the network that should be protected and which measures can be taken against attackers.

With the popularity of OAuth 2.0 and the flexibility it offers, which resulted in various implementations of authorization servers and client applications and increased knowledge, a new RFC document was published by the IETF named *OAuth 2.0 Threat Model and Security Considerations*, with its sole purpose being to inform and educate users about the additional security considerations they should have in mind.

This chapter is based on information related to security outlined in the OAuth 2.0 specification, and additionally on the information provided from this threat model RFC (RFC 6819 to be precise).

First, we'll learn what data is to be protected and what can happen if it's not, then about the security features OAuth 2.0 provides, and in the end we'll learn which security considerations we can take into account in order to build more secure applications.

What is there to be protected

The amount of data that is transmitted during the execution of an OAuth2.0 grant flow is not to be undervalued. Various parameters are in use when performing requests and responses, and some of them contain information that can be used maliciously if obtained by attackers.

Different parameters can be used by attackers for different goals:

- The client identifier and secret can be used to impersonate the original client application
- The access token can be used to access protected resources on behalf of the user and perform harmful operations on them (such as modification or deletion)
- The refresh token, together with the client credentials, can be used to issue a new access token
- And last but not least, the resource owner's username and password can be used by the attacker in various malicious ways

If not properly secured, the protected resources can be compromised and various security risks can be introduced.

OAuth 2.0 security features

OAuth 2.0 provides several features that are a part of the protocol and are related to improving security and dealing with attacks. We'll explore them one by one, by briefly explaining what each feature does, and what purpose it serves regarding security.

Scope

In the various authorization grant flows we encountered the parameter scope, which is used by the clients to specify in the request which type of access is to be granted to them on behalf of the resource owner, and is used by authorization servers in the response to confirm the same.

When an access token is issued to a client application, the scope specified in it defines the access authorization associated for that particular token. It defines which resources and API methods on these resources the client application can access and execute with the given access token.

Security wise, with scope in OAuth2.0 we can:

- Reduce the type of access from the client application to the resource server to the level that is really needed
- Minimize the damage an attacker can perform if an access token is stolen
- Have an overview of the API methods that are accessible by a client with a given token

Additionally, also for damage minimization, the client application can request a lesser scope than the one already granted for its access token.

Token lifetime

Another protocol parameter is `expires_in`, which we receive as a part of the response from the authorization server when the client application requests an access token. This parameter states the lifetime of the issued access token in seconds, and if the value of this lifetime is small they are called short-lived access tokens.

Security wise, this parameter is used to limit the duration of the lifetime so that stolen tokens will have less time to be abused in doing damaging actions. The less secure the client application is, the more short-lived the access token received by the authorization server should be. The same applies for tokens sent over non-secure channels.

The refresh token

The refresh token is a parameter, named `refresh_token`, that is also received as a part of the response from the authorization server when the client application requests an access token. Except for the client credentials grant, where it is explicitly excluded, in all grant flows defined in OAuth 2.0 it is an optional parameter that can be included in the response from the authorization server.

The purpose of the refresh token is to give the client application the possibility of renewing (or in other words, to refresh) the expired access token without redoing the whole grant flow from the start. It can ask the authorization server directly to issue a new access token.

The refresh token is mapped to the particular client application for which it was granted together with the access token. This means an access token can be renewed only with the same client credentials that were used when it was retrieved.

From a security standpoint, the use of refresh tokens:

- Helps in minimizing the involvement of end-user input by direct communication between the client and authorization server. This results in fewer spots that can be vulnerable or attacked and also results in less data being transmitted over the network.
- Combines well with the use of short-lived access tokens, resulting in a good security practice where the client again can have lengthy access to protected resources, but by refreshing several access tokens.

Related to refresh tokens, the OAuth 2.0 specification also mandates:

- That the confidentiality of refresh tokens must be maintained by the client application
- That the refresh tokens are transmitted from/to the authorization server only by using TLS
- That the authorization server will implement techniques against attackers such as guessing refresh tokens

Authorization code

When using the authorization code grant, we learned that first the end user has to approve the authorization request, usually in some web interface; after that the authorization server sends an authorization code to the client application, and after that this code is used by the client to request an access token (and optionally a refresh token).

After a successful end user authorization process, the authorization code is sent to the client's redirect URI (also called callback URI).

The authorization code grant is a browser-based redirection flow, meaning a web interface is opened in the browser or as a component in a desktop or mobile application, in which the end user has to approve or deny the authorization request. Attackers can try to access the URI parameters, the browser cache, and so on.

Due to this fact, we have the following security precautions:

- Instead of sending the access token, the authorization code is sent first, as an intermediary.
- The authorization code has a very short lifetime.
- After the client application has retrieved the authorization code, when requesting the access token with it, it is authenticated by the authorization server. This authentication is more secure and simple because it is performed directly.

Redirect URI

The redirect URI parameter, also called callback, and named `redirect_uri` in the protocol, is used by the client application to specify to the authorization server which address to return any information to when processing its request.

It is used in the authorization code grant, to hand over the authorization code on this URI back to the client, and in the implicit grant to hand over an access token in the same manner.

The main purpose of the redirect URI is preventing phishing attacks (for example, a compromised client application changes the URI to point in some other direction in order that the attacker gets the authorization code). In order to prevent this:

- It is a common practice for application developers to have to specify the redirect URIs when performing application registration. This way, when the client application specifies a URI that is not one of those pre-registered, the request will fail. This is especially important when using the implicit grant.

- When using the authorization code grant, the client specifies the redirect URI in the request for the authorization code and it has to specify the same URI again when requesting the access token. If these two URIs are not the same, the request will fail.

State

The protocol parameter named `state` is used in the authorization code and implicit grant types. It's an optional parameter that can be specified in the request for the authorization server, and closely related to the redirect URI parameter, which is specified in the request as well.

The behavior of this parameter is simple: when creating the request we add this parameter and specify some predefined value for it, for example, some random hexadecimal string or some session value, and when the server returns a response to the redirect URI, the value in the `state` parameter should be the same. In short, with this parameter the state between the request and the callback is maintained.

The main purpose of this parameter is to protect against **cross-site request forgery (CSRF)**. If the returned value for this parameter is not the same as the one in the request, and it's not due to a server error, it means that:

- The attacker has intercepted and modified the flow

- The authorization code and/or the access token can have been stolen

- The attacker has maliciously accessed protected resources and methods on behalf of the user

If any of this scenario occurs, we should check for suspicious access tokens that have been issued and revoke them immediately.

Client identifier

In all OAuth2.0 grants, when performing the grant flow, for the request from the client application to be processed, among other checks and validations the identity of the client has to be verified. For this to happen, the client application specifies in the request parameters its identifier and secret, named in the protocol as `client_id` and `client_secret`.

Securitywise, the use of client identifiers

- Provides the resource owner (the end user) with information about the identity of the client application that is requesting approval.

- Provides the authorization server means to determine whether the client application is already registered and if it has the rights to initiate a given OAuth2.0 grant flow. For example, if the client application is of type public (cannot keep the credentials confidential), the authorization server can deny initiation of all OAuth2.0 grant flows except for the implicit grant.

- Allows the authorization server to make several securitywise associations in order to use them for security checks, such as which access tokens and which access codes are issued to which clients. After that the authorization server also associates authorization codes with redirect URIs and so on.

Security considerations

One general piece of advice that applies to every type of application development is to develop the software with security in mind, meaning it is more expensive for an error-prone application to first implement the needed features and after that to make modifications in them to enforce security. Instead, this should be done simultaneously.

In this chapter we are raising security awareness, and next we will learn about which measures we can apply and what we can do in order to have more secure applications.

Use TLS

TLS (the cryptographic protocol named **Transport Layer Security**) is the result of the standardization of the SSL protocol (Version 3.0), which was developed by Netscape and was proprietary. Thus, in various documents and specifications, we can find the use of TLS and SSL interchangeably, even though there are actually differences in the protocol.

From a security standpoint, it is recommended that all requests sent from the client during the execution of a grant flow are done over TLS. In fact, it is recommended TLS be used on both sides of the connection.

OAuth 2.0 relies heavily on TLS; this is done in order to maintain confidentiality of the exchanged data over the network by providing encryption and integrity on top of the connection between the client and server. In retrospect, in OAuth 1.0 the use of TLS was not mandatory, and parts of the authorization flow (on both server side and client side) had to deal with cryptography, which resulted in various implementations, some good and some sloppy.

When we make an HTTP request (for example, in order to execute some OAuth 2.0 grant flow), in order to make the connection secure the HTTP client library that is used to execute the request has to be configured to use TLS.

TLS is to be used by the client application when sending requests to both authorization and resource servers, and is to be used by the servers themselves as well. The result is an end-to-end TLS protected connection. If end-to-end protection cannot be established, it is advised to reduce the scope and lifetime of the access tokens that are issued by the authorization server.

The OAuth2.0 specification states that the use of TLS is mandatory when sending requests to the authorization and token endpoints and when sending requests using password authentication. Access tokens, refresh tokens, username and password combinations, and client credentials must be transmitted with the use of TLS.

By using TLS, the attackers that are trying to intercept/eavesdrop the exchanged information during the execution of the grant flow will not be able to do so. If TLS is not used, attackers can eavesdrop on an access token, an authorization code, a username and password combination, or other critical information.

This means that the use of TLS prevents man-in-the-middle attacks and replaying of already fulfilled requests (also called replay attacks). By performing replay attempts, the attackers can issue themselves new access tokens or can perform replays on a request towards resource servers and modify or delete data belonging to the resource owner.

Last but not least, the authorization server can enforce the use of TLS on every endpoint in order to reduce the risk of phishing attacks.

Ensure web server application protection

For client applications that are actually web applications deployed on a server, there are numerous protection measures that can be taken into account so that the server, the database, and the configuration files are kept safe.

The list is not limited and can vary between scenarios and environments; some of the key measures are as follows:

- Install recommended security additions and tools for the given web and database servers that are in use.

- Restrict remote administrator access only to the people that require it (for example, for server maintenance and application monitoring).

- Regulate which server user can have which roles, and regulate permissions for the resources available to them.

- Disable or remove unnecessary services on the server.

- Regulate the database connections so that they are only available to the client application.

- Close unnecessary open ports on the server; leaving them open can give an advantage to the attacker.

- Configure protection against SQL injection.

- Configure database and file encryption for vital information stored (credentials and so on). Avoid storing credentials in plain text format.

- Keep the software components that are in use updated in order to avoid security exploitation.

- Avoid security misconfiguration.

It is important to have in mind what kind of web server it is, which database is used, which modules the client application uses, and on which services the client application depends, so that we can research how to apply the security measures appropriately.

OWASP (Open Web Application Security Project) provides additional documentation on security measures and describes the industry's best practices regarding software security. It is an additional resource recommended for reference and research on this topic, and can be found at `https://www.owasp.org`.

Ensure mobile and desktop application protection

Mobile and desktop applications can be installed on devices and machines that can be part of internal/enterprise or external environments. They are more vulnerable compared to the applications deployed on regulated server environments. Attackers have a better chance to try to extract the source code from the applications and other data that comes with them.

In order to provide the best possible security, some of the key measures are as follows:

- Use secure storage mechanisms provided by additional programming libraries and by features offered by the operating system for which the application is developed.

- In multiuser operating systems, store user specific data such as credentials or access and refresh tokens in locations that are not available to other users on the same system.

- As mentioned previously, credentials should not be stored in plain text format and should be encrypted.

- If using an embedded database (such as SQLite in most cases), try to enforce security measures against SQL injection and encrypt the vital information (or encrypt the whole embedded database).

- For mobile devices, advise the end user to utilize device lock (usually with a PIN, password, or face unlock).

- Implement an optional PIN or password lock on the application level that the end user can activate if desired (which can also serve as an alternative to the previous locking measure).

- Sanitize and validate the value from any input fields that are used in the applications, in order to avoid code injection, which can lead to changing the behavior or exposeing data stored by the client application.

- When the application is ready to be packaged for production use (to be used by end users), perform code analysis for obfuscating code and removing the unused code. This will produce a smaller client application in file size, which will perform the same but it will be harder to reverse engineer.

As usual, for additional reference and research we can refer to the OAuth2.0 threat model RFC document, to OWASP, and to security documentation specific to the programming language, tools, libraries, and operating system that the client application is built for.

Utilize the state parameter

As mentioned, with this parameter the state between the request and the callback is maintained. Even if it is an optional parameter it is highly advisable to use, and the value from the callback response will be validated if it is equal to the one that was sent.

When setting the value for the state parameter in the request

- Don't use predictable values that can be guessed by attackers.

- Don't repeat the same value often between requests.

- Don't use values that can contain and expose some internal business logic of the system and can be used maliciously if discovered.

- Use session values: If the user agent—with which the user has authenticated and approved the authorization request—has its session cookie available, calculate a hash from it and use that one as the state value.

- Or use some string generator: If a session variable is not available as an alternative, we use some generated programmable value. Some real world implementations do this by generating unique identifiers and using them as state values, commonly achieved by generating a random **UUID** (**universally unique identifier**) and converting it to a hexadecimal value.

- Keep track of which state value was set for which request (user session in most cases) and redirect URI, in order to validate that the returned one contains an equal value.

Use refresh tokens when available

For client applications that have obtained an access token and a refresh token along with it, upon access token expiry it is a good practice to request a new one by using the refresh token instead of going through the whole grant flow again.

With this measure we are transmitting less data over the network and are providing less exposure that the attacker can monitor.

Request the needed scope only

As briefly mentioned previously in this chapter, it is highly advisable to specify only the required scope when requesting an access token instead of specifying the maximum one that is available.

With this measure, if an attacker gets hold of the access token, he can take damaging actions only to the level specified by the scope, and not more. This is done for damage minimization until the token is revoked and invalidated.

Summary

In this chapter we learned what data is to be protected, what features OAuth 2.0 contains regarding information security, and which precautions we should take into consideration.

In the next chapter we will go a step further, and learn about SAML 2.0 bearer assertion in OAuth 2.0, as a means of providing additional security when doing client authentication or requesting an access token.

9
Additional Security with SAML

In the previous chapter we started dealing with security. We learned that the data that is transmitted during the execution of a grant flow should be treated with security in mind. We learned about the features that are part of the OAuth 2.0 specification which are related to information security, and most importantly we learned which precautions should be taken into consideration.

OAuth 2.0 offers a wide array of available authorization grant types, and also allows defining new ones, which is useful when you need to integrate with some existing security protocol. Furthermore, OAuth 2.0 also allows defining additional authentication mechanisms.

In this chapter we will learn how to use SAML 2.0 assertions for adding additional security, either as a way of doing client authentication or as an authorization grant. More specifically, we will learn what an OAuth 2.0 assertion is, what SAML is all about, and how the access token grant and authentication are done with SAML 2.0 bearer assertion.

SAML (2.0)

SAML (Security Assertion Markup Language), is an XML-based protocol that is used for exchanging authentication and authorization data for a given principal (usually an end user) between SAML identity providers and service providers.

SAML 2.0 mainly solves two requirements that are common in large enterprises:

- Web-based single sign-on across multiple domains
- Federated identity

The combination of using SAML and OAuth 2.0 together means leveraging SAML identity providers and providing easier integration in environments where SAML is already in use.

OAuth 2.0 assertions

To have a general framework for using assertions in OAuth 2.0, a separate RFC specification referred to as OAuth Assertion Framework is being developed, which outlines the following:

- A framework for the use of assertions as authorization grants
- A framework for the use of assertions as client credentials

 Assertions can be used for both scenarios in combination or separately.

The latest draft can be found at `https://tools.ietf.org/html/draft-ietf-oauth-assertions-12`.

Based on this specification, which defines message flows and the processing rules in an abstract way, another specification is being developed specifically for the use of SAML 2.0 assertions. The latest draft of this specification can be found at `https://tools.ietf.org/html/draft-ietf-oauth-saml2-bearer-17`.

These two specifications are still not final, it's safe to say they are stable, and there are already companies such as Salesforce.com and Ping Identity that have done practical implementations of them and are part of the specification development. These implementations are available and can be utilized by client application developers.

So, what are assertions? The Assertion Framework specification puts it this way:

> *An assertion is a package of information that facilitates the sharing of identity and security information across security domains.*

This package of information is actually an XML security token. The assertion, in the form of statement, asserts security information about a subject and additionally defines conditions to these statements or to (the assertion) itself.

Main components of an assertion are statements, conditions, and the subject. For example, a SAML assertion can state that a user with the e-mail address `user@example.com` is part of the bloggers company group, and that the assertion itself is valid for a fixed period of time (defined with a starting and ending point).

There are three kinds of statements that can be defined in an assertion:

- Authentication statements
- Attribute statements
- Authorization decision statements

Other assertion based specifications

It is worth mentioning that, besides the OAuth SAML Assertion Profiles specification, another one is developed as well, referred to as OAuth JWT Assertion Profiles, which outlines the use of JSON Web Tokens for requesting access tokens and client authentication.

It is based on the same Assertion Framework specification and it's pretty similar in style; the latest draft can be found at `http://tools.ietf.org/html/draft-ietf-oauth-jwt-bearer-06`.

OAuth 2.0 SAML bearer assertion grant flow

Here we'll explore how SAML 2.0 bearer assertions can be used as authorization grants.

Regarding bearer assertions: a bearer is an entity (for example, a client application) in possession of an assertion, where the entity doesn't have to demonstrate proof of possession of the given assertion with some cryptographic key. Because of this, when the client application is supplying the assertion in the request to the server, the use of secure communication (TLS) is required so that the assertion is not compromised.

Key characteristic of this new grant type is that the client application is exchanging the SAML assertion for an access token.

The flow consists of the following steps:

1. The grant flow is initiated (on behalf of the end user or by some task) by the client application.
2. The client application either generates a SAML assertion or obtains it from a SAML identity provider.
3. The client application makes an HTTP POST request to the authorization server in order to exchange the assertion.

4. The authorization server performs client authorization and validation of the supplied data from the request. If the application is authorized and the assertion is validated the server returns an access token; if any error occurred during the process, an error response is returned.

If we illustrate the flow we get the following diagram:

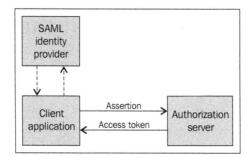

Bear in mind that before the flow is initiated, the application has to be registered. Registration is a process that is described in *Chapter 3, First Step for Your Application*. In this scenario the user additionally has to register an X.509 Certificate. If certificate registration is required it should be specified in the registration interface provided by the authorization server.

Preparing assertion

In order to prepare the SAML 2.0 assertion XML we need to have the values of the following XML attributes and elements:

- `Issuer`: This is the location of the SAML identity provider (for example, `https://saml-idp.example-service.com`), or the OAuth 2.0 client's `client_id` field.

- `NameID`: This is a field inside the parent element named `Subject`. It contains an e-mail address of the user on whose behalf the flow is initiated (for example, `test-user@example.com`).

- `Audience`: This is used for specifying a URI reference for where the assertion is intended for (for example, `https://saml-sp.example-service.net`).

- `Recipient`: This is an attribute for the `SubjectConfirmationData` element, specifying the authorization server's token endpoint URI on which the POST request will be executed (for example, `https://example-service.com/oauth/token`).

- `NotOnOrAfter`: This is an attribute for the `Conditions` element, specifying the expiration date until which the assertion can be used. This field can be used for the `SubjectConfirmationData` element as well; it must be specified in at least one of these elements.

- `NotBefore`: This is an optional attribute that can be used in the same places as the `NotOnOrAfter` attribute, specifying from which point in time the assertion can be used.

When these fields are prepared, additionally the assertion must be digitally signed using the standardized XML Signature W3C specification, and this data goes into the `Signature` element of the assertion. The signature can be signed with RSA, SHA-1, or SHA-256, all supported in popular programming languages.

Following is an example, taken and adjusted from the specification, of a prepared assertion:

```
<Assertion IssueInstant="2010-10-01T20:07:34.619Z"
  ID="ef1xsbZxPV2oqjd7HTLRLIBlBb7"
  Version="2.0"
  xmlns="urn:oasis:names:tc:SAML:2.0:assertion">
<Issuer>https://saml-idp.example-service.com</Issuer>
<ds:Signature xmlns:ds="http://www.w3.org/2000/09/xmldsig#">
  [...omitted for brevity...]
</ds:Signature>
<Subject>
  <NameID
  Format="urn:oasis:names:tc:SAML:1.1:nameid-format:emailAddress">
    test-user@example.com
  </NameID>
  <SubjectConfirmation
  Method="urn:oasis:names:tc:SAML:2.0:cm:bearer">
    <SubjectConfirmationData
    NotOnOrAfter="2010-10-01T20:12:34.619Z"
    Recipient="https://example-service.com/oauth/token"/>
  </SubjectConfirmation>
</Subject>
<Conditions>
<AudienceRestriction>
  <Audience>https://saml-sp.example-service.net</Audience>
</AudienceRestriction>
</Conditions>
<AuthnStatement AuthnInstant="2010-10-01T20:07:34.371Z">
<AuthnContext>
  <AuthnContextClassRef>
```

```
        urn:oasis:names:tc:SAML:2.0:ac:classes:X509
      </AuthnContextClassRef>
    </AuthnContext>
    </AuthnStatement>
  </Assertion>
```

One last thing to do is to encode the whole assertion by using base64url encoding before adding it as part of the POST request.

Requesting authorization

Now that we have the assertion prepared, it's time to prepare the POST request in order to execute it.

The endpoint with the required parameters may have the following form:

```
https://example-service.com/oauth/token?grant_
type=urn:ietf:params:oauth:grant-type:saml2-bearer&assertion=Assertio
nToBase64Url
```

The parameters that are used when constructing the request are the following:

- `grant_type`: This is a mandatory parameter, always set to `urn:ietf:params:oauth:grant-type:saml2-bearer`

- `assertion`: This is a mandatory parameter, contains a single SAML 2.0 assertion encoded with the base64url method

- `scope`: This is an optional parameter, used for specifying which parts (or types) of protected resources can be accessed on behalf of the owner

- `client_id`: This is an optional parameter, used for client identification

- `client_secret`: This is an optional parameter, used for client identification

Successful authorization

If the client is authenticated and the supplied fields and assertions are validated, the authorization server will respond with an access token.

The body of the response may have the following form:

```
{
  "access_token":"exampleAccessTokenValue123",
  "expires_in":3600
}
```

Note that refresh tokens usually are not issued when using this grant type. Client applications can try to refresh the expired access token by requesting a new one with the same assertion. If the assertion has expired then a new access token can be requested by executing the whole grant flow from the start.

Authorization error

If the assertion is not valid or has expired, the authorization server returns a response containing information regarding the error.

```
{
  "error":"invalid_grant",
  "error_description":"Audience validation failed",
  "error_uri":https://example-service.com/docs/oauth/saml
}
```

The value of the `error` parameter will always be `invalid_grant`. The value in the `error_description` may contain a short message relating to why the assertion failed, and optionally the parameter `error_uri` may be included, which contains a link to a web document containing more detailed explanation.

To know in detail which validation steps the authorization server takes when it receives an assertion, check the *Assertion Format and Processing Requirements* section of the OAuth SAML Assertion Profiles draft specification.

OAuth 2.0 SAML assertions for client authentication

When using one of the grants defined in OAuth 2.0, SAML assertions can be used for providing client authentication. When the authorization server processes the access token request in a given grant flow, it will check whether the client's credentials are valid based on the assertion, and then the client will be authorized to make the request.

The structure of the assertion XML is the same as in the previous case, with the difference that it's not used in exchange for an access token; it's purpose is to provide client identification information.

When using assertions for client authentication, the way the assertion is obtained from the SAML identity provider is not part of the specification and may differ between implementations, so always check the developer documentation provided for the given provider.

Requesting the access token

We will make a request for the access token using the authorization code grant from the point where the client application has already requested and obtained the authorization code and will request the access token next.

The endpoint with the required parameters may have the following form:

```
https://example-service.com/oauth/token?grant_type=authorization_
code&code=AUTHORIZATION_CODE_VALUE&client_assertion_type=urn%3Aietf%3
Aparams%3Aoauth%3Aclient-assertion-type%3Asaml2-bearer&assertion=Asse
rtionToBase64Url
```

The parameters that are used when constructing the request are the following:

- `grant_type`: This is a mandatory parameter, in our example `authorization_code`
- `client_assertion`: This is a mandatory parameter containing a single SAML 2.0 assertion encoded with the base64url method
- `client_assertion_type`: This is a mandatory parameter, always set to `urn:ietf:params:oauth:client-assertion-type:saml2-bearer`

Next, we check the parameters from the chosen grant, so in our case additional parameters in the request are:

- `code`: This is the authorization code previously retrieved from the authorization server
- `redirect_uri`: This is where the authorization server should redirect the client and supply the access token
- `client_id`: This is an optional parameter, used for client identification
- `client_secret`: This is an optional parameter, used for client identification

Authentication error

If the assertion is not valid, for any reason, the authorization server returns a response containing information regarding the error:

```
{
   "error":"invalid_client"
}
```

The value of the `error` parameter in this case will always be `invalid_client`. Optionally, the parameters `error_message` and `error_uri` may be included.

Note that the validation of the assertion is the same as in the previous case.

Summary

In this chapter we learned about SAML 2.0 bearer assertions in OAuth 2.0, as a means of providing additional security when doing client authentication or when requesting an access token.

In the next chapter, we will cover the tools and libraries available for client developers, so that we have an overview of which of the popular programming languages have which libraries to ease the development process.

10
Common Tools and Libraries

In the previous chapter, we learned about SAML 2.0 bearer assertion in OAuth 2.0, as a means of providing additional security when doing client authentication or when requesting an access token.

In this chapter, the last one of this book, we will cover the tools and libraries available for client developers. It is divided into two parts. First, we'll cover the tools, given their platform-neutral nature, and after that we'll cover the libraries that the developers can use for their chosen programming language and environment.

The idea is that client developers, having knowledge of various OAuth 2.0 grant flows and of the security considerations, choose the appropriate grant for a given scenario and then either implement the grant flow on their own, or choose a library for the programming language in which the application is (to be) written. By choosing a library for handling OAuth 2.0, the client developer may save some time during the development process, but may lack the possibility to do some customizations.

Tools

Various tools are made available to the client developers by OAuth2.0. We will have a brief overview of each of these tools in the following sections.

OAuth 2.0 Playground

The OAuth 2.0 Playground is a web tool made by Google, providing developers with means to test various OAuth 2.0 grants together with the various Google APIs that support OAuth 2.0.

This tool can be found at `https://developers.google.com/oauthplayground/`.

RESTClient

RESTClient is a browser extension (for Firefox) for testing RESTful web services that use OAuth 2.0.

This tool can be found at `http://restclient.net/`.

Postman

Postman is another browser extension (for Chrome) for testing RESTful web services that use OAuth 2.0.

This tool can be found at `http://www.getpostman.com/`.

Libraries

In this book, in the various code examples, we didn't use a library specifically for OAuth 2.0, but instead used the Spring framework MVC controllers to map endpoints and extract the parameters, the Apache HTTP client to make requests to the authorization servers, and the GSON library to parse the JSON files retuned by them.

This way, we implemented the various OAuth 2.0 grant flows by ourselves, and by doing that we showed what is going on under the hood. By implementing the various OAuth 2.0 grant flows by ourselves, we are able to modify the code in the client application faster and more easily, if the flow is not 100 percent by specification but has some customization to it.

Nevertheless, there are numerous libraries for various popular programming languages, which can be used to ease the use of OAuth 2.0 in either client applications or server-side applications to provide OAuth 2.0 compliant services.

We'll list the libraries sorted by programming language, in alphabetical order, and name one or a few of the most popular ones for each language.

These are the most popular libraries at the given moment. As technology and time moves forward sometimes new libraries emerge, providing more optimal or fully-featured implementations.

C#

The most popular library that supports OAuth 2.0 and can be used when building client applications is `DotNetOpenAuth`.

This library can be found at `http://dotnetopenauth.net/`.

Clojure

For Clojure, there is `friend-oauth2`, which is used together with `Friend`, a library for authentication and authorization used in Clojure ring-based web applications and services. It is used for adding authentication and authorization for web applications and services with OAuth 2.0.

This library can be found at `https://github.com/cemerick/friend/`.

Another common choice is `oauth-clj`, which is used for building client applications and can be found at `https://github.com/r0man/oauth-clj/`.

Go

For Google's new programming language named Go, there is a library available called `goauth2` and it's used for building client applications.

This library can be found at `https://code.google.com/p/goauth2/`.

Java

For Java there are several libraries; among them are Spring Security and Spring Social, Apache Oltu, and of course Scribe. Spring Security and Oltu are used on the server side to implement authorization and resource servers, and Spring Social and Scribe are used on the client side for building client applications.

These libraries can be found at the following URLs:

- `http://projects.spring.io/spring-social/`
- `http://projects.spring.io/spring-security/`
- `https://oltu.apache.org/`
- `https://github.com/fernandezpablo85/scribe-java/`

JavaScript

The usual way is to use jQuery's AJAX support, as we have done in the example in *Chapter 5*, *OAuth for Client-side Applications*.

When OAuth 1.0 was finalized, there were some JavaScript libraries specifically targeting OAuth, but with the deprecation of OAuth 1.0 and the emergence of OAuth 2.0, these libraries didn't upgrade or did but are not stable. Therefore, there are none to recommend.

Facebook, Google, and others provide their own JavaScript libraries. They can be found at the following URLs:

- `https://developers.facebook.com/docs/reference/javascript/`
- `https://developers.google.com/api-client-library/javascript/features/authentication/`

Objective-C

One option is to use **Google Toolbox for Mac** OAuth 2.0 controllers, simply called **GTM**; and another one is AFOAuth2Client, which is an extension for the AFNetworking networking library. Both are used for building client applications.

They can be found at the following URLs:

- `https://code.google.com/p/gtm-oauth2/`
- `https://github.com/AFNetworking/AFOAuth2Client/`

Perl

Perl offers several libraries as well, among them are Net-OAuth2 and p5-oauth-lite2. They are both used for building client applications, and the second one is used additionally for building authorization and resource servers.

They can be found at the following URLs:

- `https://github.com/keeth/Net-OAuth2/`
- `https://github.com/lyokato/p5-oauth-lite2/`

PHP

PHP is rich in choice as the other languages, where `PHP-OAuth2` and `oauth2-client` appear to be commonly used, both offering simplicity. For those using the CodeIgniter PHP framework, a separate library is available as well. All of them are used for building client applicaions.

They can be found on the following URLs:

- `https://github.com/adoy/PHP-OAuth2/`
- `https://github.com/php-loep/oauth2-client/`
- `https://github.com/philsturgeon/codeigniter-oauth2/`

Python

For Python, `rauth` seems to be one of the most popular libraries, and for those using the Django framework `django-socialregistration` is available as well. Both are used for building client applications.

They can be found at the following URLs:

- `https://github.com/litl/rauth/`
- `https://github.com/flashingpumpkin/django-socialregistration/`

Ruby

For Ruby (and JRuby and Rubinius) the most popular choice is the generically named library `oauth2` used for building client applications.

This library can be found at `https://github.com/intridea/oauth2/`

Scala

For Scala, for the users of the popular Play framework, there is a library called `securesocial`, and additionally there is a framework-independent Scala library called `joauth`. Both are used for building client applications.

They can be found at the following URLs:

- `https://github.com/jaliss/securesocial/`
- `https://github.com/twitter/joauth/`

Summary

In this chapter, we have covered the tools and libraries related to OAuth 2.0, available for client developers.

This is also the last chapter of the book, and next is the *Appendix, OAuth 2.0 Resources*, containing pointers to resources handy for everyone interested in further expanding their knowledge of OAuth 2.0 or getting involved in future specification development.

OAuth 2.0 Resources

In the last chapter we reviewed which tools and libraries are available for application developers to utilize when building an OAuth client application.

This appendix is a compilation of resources ranging from RFC documents to websites and mailing lists, handy for everyone interested in further expanding their knowledge or getting involved in future specification development.

OAuth 2.0 specification

The OAuth 2.0 specification, fully named The OAuth 2.0 Authorization Framework, is an RFC publication, developed by the **Internet Engineering Task Force (IETF)**. It is a proposed standard (an Internet Standards Track document) and it deprecates the previous OAuth 1.0 specification.

It is published as RFC 6749 and is available at `http://tools.ietf.org/html/rfc6749`.

OAuth WG mailing list

The official OAuth working group mailing list is maintained by the IETF.

The list archive (for browsing and reading) is available at `http://www.ietf.org/mail-archive/web/oauth/current/maillist.html`.

To subscribe to the mailing list refer to `https://www.ietf.org/mailman/listinfo/oauth`.

OAuth 2.0 Threat Model and Security Considerations

This document is also an RFC publication, outlining additional security considerations regarding OAuth 2.0. It also outlines assumptions, threats, and considerations to be taken against them.

It is not an Internet Standards Track specification, as is the OAuth 2.0 specification itself, but it is also published for informational purposes.

It is published as RFC 6819 and is available at `http://tools.ietf.org/html/rfc6819`.

The OAuth 2.0 Authorization Framework - Bearer Token Usage

This is also an RFC publication, an Internet Standards Track document, outlining how to use bearer tokens in HTTP requests to access OAuth 2.0 protected resources.

It is published as RFC 6750 and is available at `https://tools.ietf.org/html/rfc6750`.

Assertion Framework for OAuth 2.0 Client Authentication and Authorization Grants

This is an RFC draft, not finalized and still under active development, outlining a framework for how assertions can be used as authorization grants and as client credentials.

It is currently at Version 12 and can be found at `https://tools.ietf.org/html/draft-ietf-oauth-assertions-12`.

SAML 2.0 Profile for OAuth 2.0 Client Authentication and Authorization Grants

This is an RFC draft (just like the previous one), outlining the use of SAML 2.0 bearer assertion in OAuth 2.0 for both client authentication and access token request.

It is currently at version 17 and can be found at `http://tools.ietf.org/html/draft-ietf-oauth-saml2-bearer-17`.

OAuth website

Last but not least, the OAuth website, with its section on OAuth 2.0 can be found at `http://oauth.net/2/`.

Index

T

temporarily_unavailable parameter 49
TLS
  about 26, 82
  using 83
token endpoint 20
token lifetime
  reducing, for security purposes 79
tokenRequest variable 40
token_type parameter 48, 64
Transport Layer Security. *See* TLS

U

unauthorized_client parameter 49
unsupported_response_type parameter 49
URL identifier key 57
URL schemes key 57

URL Types key 57
User agent 30
user_id parameter 18, 75
username parameter 63
userName variable 38
UUID (universally unique identifier) 86

W

web server application
  protection, ensuring 84

Z

Zendesk 68, 69

Thank you for buying
OAuth 2.0 Identity and Access Management Patterns

About Packt Publishing

Packt, pronounced 'packed', published its first book "*Mastering phpMyAdmin for Effective MySQL Management*" in April 2004 and subsequently continued to specialize in publishing highly focused books on specific technologies and solutions.

Our books and publications share the experiences of your fellow IT professionals in adapting and customizing today's systems, applications, and frameworks. Our solution based books give you the knowledge and power to customize the software and technologies you're using to get the job done. Packt books are more specific and less general than the IT books you have seen in the past. Our unique business model allows us to bring you more focused information, giving you more of what you need to know, and less of what you don't.

Packt is a modern, yet unique publishing company, which focuses on producing quality, cutting-edge books for communities of developers, administrators, and newbies alike. For more information, please visit our website: www.packtpub.com.

About Packt Open Source

In 2010, Packt launched two new brands, Packt Open Source and Packt Enterprise, in order to continue its focus on specialization. This book is part of the Packt Open Source brand, home to books published on software built around Open Source licences, and offering information to anybody from advanced developers to budding web designers. The Open Source brand also runs Packt's Open Source Royalty Scheme, by which Packt gives a royalty to each Open Source project about whose software a book is sold.

Writing for Packt

We welcome all inquiries from people who are interested in authoring. Book proposals should be sent to author@packtpub.com. If your book idea is still at an early stage and you would like to discuss it first before writing a formal book proposal, contact us; one of our commissioning editors will get in touch with you.

We're not just looking for published authors; if you have strong technical skills but no writing experience, our experienced editors can help you develop a writing career, or simply get some additional reward for your expertise.

HTML5 iPhone Web Application Development

ISBN: 978-1-84969-102-4   Paperback: 338 pages

An introduction to web-application development for mobile within the iOS Safari browser

1. Simple and complex problems will be covered with examples and resources that backup the approach and technique.

2. Real world solutions that are broken down for multiple target audiences; from beginner developers to technical architects.

3. Learn to build true web applications using the latest industry standards for iOS Safari.

Symfony 1.3 Web Application Development

ISBN: 978-1-847194-56-5   Paperback: 228 pages

Design, develop, and deploy feature-rich, high-performance PHP web applications using the Symfony framework

1. Create powerful web applications by leveraging the power of this Model-View-Controller-based framework

2. Covers all the new features of version 1.3 – many exciting plug-ins for you

3. Learn by doing without getting into too much theoretical detail – create a "real-life" milkshake store application

4. Includes best practices to shorten your development time and improve performance

Please check **www.PacktPub.com** for information on our titles

Real-time Web Application Development using Vert.x 2.0

ISBN: 978-1-78216-795-2   Paperback: 122 pages

An intuitive guide to building applications for the real-time web with the Vert.x platform

1. Get started with developing applications for the real-time web

2. From concept to deployment, learn the full development workflow of a real-time web application

3. Utilize the Java skills you already have while stepping up to the next level

4. Learn all the major building blocks of the Vert.x platform

SproutCore Web Application Development

ISBN: 978-1-84951-770-6   Paperback: 194 pages

Creating fast, powerful, and feature-rich web applications using the SproutCore HTML5 framework

1. Write next-gen HTML5 apps using the SproutCore framework and tools

2. Get started right away by creating a powerful application in the very first chapter

3. Build your understanding of SproutCore as you follow through the most complete reference to the framework anywhere in existence

Please check **www.PacktPub.com** for information on our titles

www.ingramcontent.com/pod-product-compliance
Lightning Source LLC
Chambersburg PA
CBHW060154060326
40690CB00018B/4103